MAKING STAGE PROPS

A PRACTICAL GUIDE

MAKING STAGE PROPS

Andy Wilson

The Crowood Press

First published in 2003 by
The Crowood Press Ltd
Ramsbury, Marlborough
Wiltshire SN8 2HR

www.crowood.com

This impression 2007
© Andy Wilson 2003

British Library Cataloguing-in-Publication Data
A catalogue record for this book is available from the British Library.

ISBN 978 1 86126 450 3

Dedication
To my Dad, who got me into making things.

Acknowledgements
With many thanks to the following individuals for their help and support: Naomi Abigail, Vanessa Cass, Peter Dean, Rachel Harrison, Sue Hudson, Steve Huttly, Chris Lewis, Alex Madden, James McNamara, Nicky Miners, Nick Peel, John Philips, Steve Ranson, Louise Rogers, Lone Schacksen, Paddy Sheehan, Sam Shortt, Edd Smith, Helen Smith, Laura Streather, Ian Taylor and Tip. Thanks also to the casts and creative teams of the productions illustrated here and the many other staff and students of the Guildhall School of Music and Drama who worked on them.

I gratefully acknowledge the award of a Grant for Independent Research Activities by the Guildhall School of Music and Drama that enabled me to devote time to this project.

Lastly, special thanks to Jacquetta May, without whose patience, encouragement and hard work this would not have been possible.

Photographs and drawings are by the author unless otherwise credited.
Front cover photograph from the 1994 Palace Theatre Watford production of *Desire Under the Elms* by Eugene O'Neill, directed by Lou Stein and designed by Norman Coates.
Photograph previous page: Putting the finishing touches to a statue for *The Winter's Tale*, GSMD, 2001.

Disclaimer
Safety is of the utmost importance in every aspect of construction work. When using tools, always closely follow the manufacturer's recommended procedures. However, the author and publisher cannot accept responsibility for any accident or injury caused by following the advice given in this book.

Typeset and designed by Shane O'Dwyer, Swindon, Wiltshire.

Printed and bound in Spain by GraphyCems, Villatuerta, Navarra

CONTENTS

1 INTRODUCTION

The task of making props for the stage falls to many different people – stage management, workshop staff and designers (as well as prop makers) in professional theatre, enthusiastic part-timers in amateur companies, and art or craft students in schools. Even broader is the range of work that may be asked of them. Certainly 'props' still include thrones, spears and scrolls, but just as 'scenery' has long been far more than flattage and backcloths, so the contemporary stage is eclectic and unpredictable in its demand for props, and any imaginable object may be required by it.

What all these people have in common (apart from a shortage of time and funds) is that they rely on materials and techniques they are familiar with and equipped for to meet all the different challenges that arise. Knowledge of materials, of how they behave and how to manipulate them is crucial to success in prop making; without it you cannot decide how to make something, calculate costs, plan your time or predict how things will work.

The difference between all these props workshops, garages or classrooms lies in the circumstances in which they operate – the budgets, equipment, expertise and prevailing production values. There is no single 'correct' way to make any prop, but many ways, each of which may be the right one in a particular context.

LEFT: *Large-scale work: flying crucifix for* **Much Ado About Nothing**, *GSMD; designer:* **Mark Bailey**; *photograph: Laurence Burns.*

Although this book includes pointers towards different ways to make things, it stops short of prescriptions for specific items ('how to make a roast goose'). Instead it looks at materials and techniques, describing and comparing many of those in use for prop making today; it aims to encourage experiment and to help you to find the roast goose that suits you. Inevitably, much from this great 'borrowing' from other crafts and industries has had to be left out for reasons of space. Reasons for such omissions include high material cost or required level of specialist skill, or simply that the way something is done for the stage is the same as in everyday life. Other areas

Who Does What?

Contemporary theatre involves a wide variety of types of company, producing an equally wide variety of work, and all going about it in their own individual way. Whatever the context, it is likely that the maker will relate to a designer or director over the appearance and function of the prop, and a production manager (or someone in that role) over its cost, schedule and technical aspects, such as safety or the space taken up in the wings. There is also usually communication through a stage manager with the rehearsal room, enabling everyone to be informed of developments there. Finally, of course, props end up in the hands of performers or as part of the environment in which they must work.

of basic technique – carpentry skills, for instance – have been only briefly referred to because so much more information than could have been included here is readily available elsewhere. The reading list points to many more specialized books about crafts and techniques that can be adapted for the stage, and the Internet is a rich and ever expanding source of information. Of course, you can only really learn practical skills by working with the materials themselves, but books and websites may help you to learn about techniques, safety issues and so on, and make informed decisions about new materials to try.

WHY MAKE?

'Properties' include objects used by performers, furnishings and other design elements. Prop makers may also work on large, scenic elements,

Small-scale work: a sample for a costume prop (top); part of a trick clock mechanism (bottom).

applying three-dimensional detail or texture, or work on small items such as spectacles or costume jewellery.

Props may be bought, borrowed or hired, but some will need to be made or altered. While the decision to use a certain prop in a show is purely artistic and rests with the director and the designer, the question of how to acquire it may also be logistic and budgetary, and is likely to involve the production manager or the stage manager and the designer – and prop maker too, if it is possible or obvious that the prop needs to be made.

There are a number of reasons for deciding to make a prop:

* It simply is not possible to acquire it in any other way. This may be because the prop in question is a stuffed tableau of a dodo locked in mortal combat with an alien, but is more likely just to be because attempts to buy, borrow or hire it have failed.
* The design is very specific in terms of dimensions or appearance. A portrait that is a likeness of one of the cast, a kite made by a ten-year-old or just a piece of furniture that has to fit into a certain space all fall into this category. Furniture that was once grand but is now old and battered can be surprisingly hard to find – hire firms keep their stock in good shape and will not appreciate your ripping out the stuffing.
* The prop has to perform some technical function or withstand rough treatment. A china Buddha is broken every night, or a chaise is upended by two dancers and climbed upon.
* It is cheaper to make than to buy or hire. In the case of a long run or tour, hire charges can often exceed the cost of making. Manufactured goods may come in a higher finish or more lavish materials than the stage requires. Making can often be the most economic option, particularly if labour costs are in some way already accounted for.

Dates set at the meeting are as follows:

Pre production meeting – Monday 4th March – 2pm
Costings deadline – Monday 11th March
Production meeting – Tuesday 19th March – 9am

There is seating facing the control room and on the SR side of the studio as if from the control room

The set is basically made up of a series of wardrobes and chests of drawers as follows:

1 = Tall wardrobe with a single door – SM to buy – entrances made through the back of this
2 = Chest of 4 drawers – SM to buy
3 = Tall double wardrobe – SM to buy – entrances made through the back of this
4 = Tall mirrored wardrobe – this tips down and turns into a bed which needs to be moveable – this is a prop make at present
5 = Tall wardrobe – SM to buy – entrances made through the back of this
6 = Chest of 4 drawers – prop make at present BUY – S.M.
7 = Tall double wardrobe – prop make at present
8 = This is a couple of sets of drawers with clothes pouring out of them which will be a make as the purpose of these is to act as a set of treads up to the platform
9 = Tall wardrobe with 2 drawers – SM to buy

On the platform there is a dressing table and a set of practical suitcases.

There also needs to be two wicker skips – fully practical – possibly capable of hiding an actor. need swivel casters + reinforcement

The floor is still to be decided – whether floorcloth or hardboard but the design is of a map.

On the opposite side of the platform to the control room is a series of dressing made up of clothes, suits, ties etc – not clear from the model. To talk about this at the pre production meeting.

No firearms will be used in this production.

There may be a 40's period feel to the costumes.
Props may come from any period.

There may be cross casting between the main house drama and the studio.

Jonathan

An initial props list for a show.

Time

Everybody's time is valuable. It is one of the most precious commodities involved in theatre, whether for the freelance professional or the unpaid amateur with a full-time job elsewhere. Learning to judge how long something will take, so that you can plan ahead or decide on the practicality of making it at all, is vital. If you want to develop this skill, keep a record of how long things take to do. How much of it is waiting time – paint drying or glue setting – when you could be doing something else, and how much is active time when you need to focus on the job in hand? Things take much longer when you are learning to do them, and any job involving new techniques or a great deal of experimentation needs extra time; once you are familiar with a task your performance of it becomes more fluent.

LEFT: *A stylized spinning wheel, which could be turned by a motor on the flying bar, typifies props so specific that they have to be made.* The Rape of Lucretia, GSMD; *designer: Francis O'Connor; photograph: Laurence Burns.*

WHAT MAKES A 'GOOD' PROP?

There is more to a prop than its appearance. Consider it from the point of view of everyone involved:

* Director and designer. Why did they decide to have it in the first place? Does it look and function as intended?
* Production manager. Is it on time and within its budget?
* Cast and stage management. Is it safe? Does it feel right, is it too heavy or too light? Is it fragile, needing careful handling or frequent repair?
* Audience. Does it look right? Does it blend in or stand out and draw their attention? Most props are not meant to do this – like film music, they work best when we do not consciously notice them.

All these questions can be applied to anything from a steam engine to a doorstop, and all are equally important measures of the success of the work.

PLANNING

Whether one prop or a list of thirty is being made for a production, the work usually needs to be costed and scheduled in advance. This may be done by managers in larger professional companies, but in smaller organizations it is likely to be done by the makers themselves.

Deciding How to Make Something

The great majority of props involve several different materials and processes in combination. A mask may be modelled in clay, a mould taken and a cast made in papier mâché; it might then be decorated with paint, sequins, feathers, fake fur or whatever. A piece of furniture may involve woodwork, modelled 'carving', upholstery and a painted finish. A chandelier might combine bent and welded steel with woodturning, resin casting and metal leaf. In each case the methods used will have been selected from a range of alternatives – 'Shall I bend some flat steel into a hoop for the band of the chandelier or use that bicycle wheel that's near enough the right size?'

How to go about making something is a complex decision that hangs on a number of factors. First, of course, there are the aesthetic and technical factors: what it must look like and be able to do, and the constraints of budget. These decisions will come from, or at least involve, the

11

director, the designer and the production manager of the show. After this, it tends to be for the maker to come up with a plan of action and get on with it, with the approval of the designer or the production manager in the case of large or important items. To do this, you will need to think through each step of the several possible ways to make something. This preconception is a vital part of the making process; it enables you to foresee problems, recognize possible short-cuts and estimate how long each part of the work will take. It is essential if you are to cost the work accurately – you cannot cost something you do not know how to make. It requires you to be familiar with your materials and to know your own abilities; if you identify a point in the process you are considering where you do not know how a material will behave, or how to achieve a certain effect, then you need to do some tests or make or acquire some samples to resolve the matter. These can also help designers to specify colours, textures or whatever.

As well as considering the budget, facilities and skills available to you and the needs of the creative team, the following questions may help you in deciding how to make something:

* How was or is such a thing really made? Even if you cannot duplicate it exactly, you may be able to find a prop equivalent – carved polystyrene for carved stone, or cast GRP for cast iron. Also, the way something is made may affect the way it looks; was it made by hand or by a machine? If the latter, can you mimic it?
* What is the visual 'essence' of the prop? Which elements are vital to it (and to the designer's concept of it) and which can be omitted or simplified?
* From what distance will the audience see it? Under what lighting conditions? Both have profound implications for the level of finish you need to achieve, the degree of detail you include and the way you present these

This moose head, which can be animated from behind the flat it is mounted on, uses a wide range of materials and techniques. The antlers are carved polystyrene, covered with muslin and epoxy resin. The head is glass-reinforced epoxy made over a clay original, finished with fake fur and flocking; the eyeballs were cast in clear polyester resin and are lit by low-voltage pea bulbs. The mechanisms that open and close the mouth and eyelids are made from wood, bent and welded steel, wire, elastic and nylon cord. Its teeth were modelled in polycaprolactone, which was also used to fix many of the other parts together. **Babes In Arms,** *GSMD; designer Mark Bailey.*

details. If you are unsure about the effects of distance and lighting, make or find some sample pieces with various amounts of detail and examine them under different kinds of lighting at a distance. When you look at your own and others' work in performance, what detail – and what flaws – can you see?

* How have other makers solved this? Many will be happy to discuss methods with you; even if their circumstances are very different from yours, they may suggest approaches you have not considered.

* How much of a risk can you afford to take? Sometimes you may have enough time (or budget) to start something without knowing quite how you are going to finish it; some problems, and their solutions, become apparent only as the work progresses. And sometimes it is better to use a material or technique you know well than an unfamiliar one that is supposedly better for the job – have you really got time to learn about it now?

Costing

An accurate costing should be done to make sure that the work can be completed within the given budget. It enables you to compare possible ways to make something, and if the production as a whole is costed over-budget, it enables production management or the creative team to make informed decisions about potential savings.

What is being costed, of course, is a particular way of making something. You cannot cost accurately if you do not know how to make it. Where you have only a rough idea how you will approach it, you can at least make estimates. Think through your intended way of making the item and list all the materials involved. Try to include secondary materials such as brushes or disposable gloves, unless they are already accounted for. Work out how much of each material you will need to buy. This will involve knowing the quantities in which it comes and possibly some mathematics or technical drawing ('Exactly how many cut-out penguins can I get from each sheet of plywood?').

When a long list of props is being costed, there may well be materials shared between them; this may reduce the quantity you need, but bear in mind that, if one item is cut, it may affect your shopping list for another. Finally, put a price to each item on the list, not forgetting things such as delivery charges, and the prop is costed. Some things may have to be estimated – an upholstery fabric that has not been chosen yet or that second-hand birdcage you are planning to adapt. Items such as screws and paint may have to be represented by a general figure at the end of your costing.

Lack of finalized information or decisions means that accurate costing is not always possible and gaps may have to be filled by estimates.

Scheduling

As you think your way through each step of making something, you should be considering the timescale as well as the cost of the work. The two are often closely related; as a general rule, the cheaper a process, the longer it seems to take. If you are worried about completing on time or your many items all have different deadlines, you need to plan carefully. Work out a miniature schedule for each item in terms of the number of hours or days each step needs. Include things such as shopping trips and drying times. Consider any appointments that have to be arranged, such as a session to take a life mould of an actor's face.

Then look at each prop from the point of view of when it needs to be finished and mark a deadline for each on a chart. Some may not be needed until the technical rehearsal. Others may have to be on stage by the time the lighting rig is focused or be attached to the set at the fit-up. Interactive props may be required in rehearsals well before the production moves on to the stage.

Finally, combine all these schedules on the chart, working back from each deadline. Although it may be a rude shock to find out how little time you have, planning in this much detail will show clearly how best to use it. As with budgeting, lack of crucial information

G.S.M.D.	Estimated Budget. Prop Makes		Opera Double Bill
ITEM	**MATERIALS**	**QUANTITY**	**COST**
Bed	1" x 3" PAR @ 0.94	40m	£37.60
	1" x 4" PAR @ 1.40	10m	£14.00
	2" x 3" PAR @ 1.83	5m	£9.15
	19mm ply @13.00	1sheet	£13.00
	4mm ply @7.64	2 sheets	£15.28
	9mm MDF @12.00	3 sheets	£36.00
	Astragal TP 610 @1.50	7m	£10.50
	Bullnose and Scotia TP 43 @1.10	2m	£2.20
	Scotia TP 355 @ 0.57	8m	£4.56
	Staff bead TP 74 @ 0.68	10m	£6.80
	70mm wooden balls @ 2.56	Four	£10.24
	TS3 075 PT03 castor @ 14.64	Eight	£117.12
	Button pelmet clips @ 2.90	Eight	£23.20
	38mm wooden knobs @ 5.00/10	Sixteen	£10.00
	Fixings, filler, paint and glaze		£20.00
		£329.65	
Cornices	1" x 3" PAR @ 0.94	5m	£4.70
	4mm ply	1 sheet	£7.64
	Vac-form (to be selected)	estimate	£20.00
	Styrofoam and Foamcoat ex stock		
	Button pelmet clips @ 2.90	Four	£11.60
		£43.94	
Curtain rails	1¼" round ERW tube	1 bar	£13.50
	Finials turned from stock		
		£13.50	
Bunting	No 4 jute sash @0.16/m	30m	£4.80
	Calico	2m	£7.70
	Paint		£10.00
	Spray glue	2 cans	£8.00
		£30.50	
Masks	Alginate 500g @ 7.03	Ten	£70.30
	Prestia 23 plaster	One bag	£7.00
	Plaster bandage	One bag	£18.18
	Thermoplastic sheet (estimate)		£90.00
	Paint, fittings, etc		£15.00
		£200.48	
Chandelier	Possible modification costs - maximum		£25.00
		£25.00	
PROP MAKES TOTAL			**£643.07**

A typical costing. Some items have been worked out in detail, while others remain estimates awaiting further clarification.

can complicate your schedule, but working back from the deadlines should indicate when that information is needed, and help you to press for decisions.

Tools and Equipment

It is quite possible to make props with a relatively limited selection of hand tools, although the fact that prop making can cover such a wide variety of crafts and materials means that the list of potentially useful items is a long one. For those starting out, the best policy is to begin with a basic toolkit for the materials you will use most (probably wood and fabrics) and to add to it only when you are sure the new addition will be useful. Some areas of work, such as modelling, moulding and casting, need few specialized tools. Others, such as metal work, require more of an investment. In each chapter I have suggested lists of the tools that are more or less essential and more 'advanced' or expensive equipment.

Machines and expensive power tools enable you either to do something you could not possibly do without them, or to do something much more quickly and effectively than is possible with hand tools. A vacuum forming machine is one of the former, and a radial arm saw one of the latter. There are also machines that do one thing only (such as a biscuit jointer) and those that are adaptable to many different tasks (such as a router).

When funds for investment are limited (that is for most of us), these more versatile tools are important. A band saw for wood and polystyrene is a prime example. Other machines that open up otherwise impossible areas of work are a lathe, a MIG welder and a sewing machine. What is best for you will depend on the type of work you do – think hard about your needs and, if possible, talk to other makers.

Workspace and Facilities

What is needed from a workspace will also vary considerably according to the work being done. The work that it is possible to do depends in turn on the nature of the space. Permanent, dedicated props workshops in professional theatres can be equipped with fixed machinery and can stock a wide variety of materials, and they can cope with the mess produced by some processes. Makers who have to share a space with other activities or who use a space only temporarily must rely on portable equipment and face greater logistical problems with storage and cleanliness.

However, it is possible to generalize that the following are desirable facilities for regular prop making:

* Ample storage space for raw materials, the work in progress and finished props. Storage can account for half your space, and in a permanent workshop may include racking for timber and steel, bins for clay and plaster, and shelving for paints and other materials. If you use flammable products you will need suitable metal cupboards. Most operations also generate large quantities of offcuts and oddments that need to be saved for a rainy day.
* A wet area (or the option to set one up) for working with messy materials such as plaster and paint. This must include a sink with a large, efficient trap and a surface for mixing.
* A dry, clean area for working with textiles – a 'softs room' or just a table well away from sawdust and plaster.
* Somewhere to do paperwork and keep drawings; if not an office, at least a desk in the corner.
* Easily cleaned surfaces and floor, a good vacuum cleaner and frequent rubbish removal.
* Last, but not least, adequate equipment to protect you and those around you from any hazards posed by the work you are doing. For instance, some processes require local exhaust ventilation or dust extraction.

Most workspaces do not have all these, but their occupants get used to the deficiencies and work around them. One essential in a workspace, though, is flexibility – the scope to adapt it to meet the changing demands of the work.

TRADITIONAL AND MODERN MATERIALS

The range of materials available to prop makers has grown immeasurably over the last few decades. A century ago, nearly everything was made from the same basics such as wood, canvas, felt, size and papier mâché. Now there is a bewildering variety of alternatives, mostly outperforming their traditional cousins: thermosetting resins, polymer paints, polystyrene and polyurethane foams, and many more. Steel entered the structural arsenal with the development of small-scale electric welding processes, while the appearance on the market of silicone 'rubber' in the 1960s revolutionized the making of moulds.

Yet all the traditional materials listed above are still in use today, because the problems that makers seek to solve have not really changed. There has always been a need to build fast, strong frameworks: wood, bamboo, steel or aluminium can all do this. Compound curved surfaces may be made from thermoplastic 'prepregs' or from felt stiffened with size. Large, shell-like structures can be produced in GRP, or, in the cliché of the props world, chicken wire and papier mâché. Materials known in ancient Egypt may be used alongside others developed only a few years ago.

The choice of a traditional material may be for economy, availability or familiarity. The modern materials perform better in one or more ways (or they would not be on the market); they are stronger, they set faster, they look better or they offer something new. Whichever you choose, and most makers end by using a mixture, what is important is to try to know them well: their possibilities and limitations, their safety, their shelf life, where best to buy them, and how to get them off your clothes.

SAFETY

Because of the diversity of materials and processes and the unpredictable scale and nature of the work, prop makers need to be particularly vigilant about health and safety.

As an employer, professional theatre is subject to legislation dealing with different aspects of health and safety at work. In the United Kingdom the Management of Health and Safety at Work Regulations oblige employers to assess the risks to which their employees (or themselves in the case of the self-employed) are exposed while at work, and the risks posed to anyone else. A range of regulations exists to cover specific aspects of health and safety, each placing further obligations on employers and employees. In this country these include the Manual Handling Operations, the Control of Substances Hazardous to Health, and the Electricity at Work Regulations. Although non-professional theatre companies and individuals may not be obliged to comply with all of these, some of the practical measures involved offer a useful framework for managing health and safety.

Risk Assessment

The key process is risk assessment. The seriousness of the hazard from a substance or operation (the damage it could potentially cause) is weighed against the likelihood of its happening; the 'risk' is the combination of these two factors. Thus an extreme hazard that is highly unlikely to happen is low risk, and a less severe hazard with a higher likelihood of occurrence may be considered a higher risk. Anything that does not come out as a negligible risk then needs to be addressed.

What is being assessed is always risk in the context of a particular process or set of circumstances. The risk of suffering the effects of styrene inhalation is far greater when using polyester resin to lay up GRP in an open mould than when pouring it into a small, closed

8. **Substances present** – to include raw materials, intermediates, products and by-products.
Please indicate the nature of the Substance(s) using the following categories:

D – dust   G – gas   V – vapour   M – mist   L – liquid   F – fume   S – solid   MB – microbiological

	Substance Type	Trade Name(s)	Components Present	Nature (dust, mist vapour etc)	Exposure Limit(s) MEL/OES	Possible routes of exposure	Approx. quantity in use	Storage facilities	Safety Data Sheets Y/N?
OK	Petroleum Jelly	Vaseline	Petroleum Jelly	L?			<200g	Shelving	N
OK	Plaster Bandage	– Gypsona – Modroc	– Calcium Sulphate Hemihydrate (– Cotton fabric)	D, becoming L then S	OEL: 10mgm³		<3Kg	In boxes beneath plaster bench	Y
	Alginate	– Scopas Dust-free Alginate – Body Alginate		D, becoming L then S			<1Kg	Shelving	Y
OK	Soap Release Agent	Mould-makers soft soap		L			<50g	Shelving	Y
needs MSDS OK	Barrier Cream	Rozalex		L			approx 15g	Shelving	Y
OK	Cleansing Cream	Resinega		L			<50g	Beside sink	Y

Part of a risk assessment form relating to life casting.

mould. Unacceptable risks must be reduced to a negligible level by changing the process or circumstances; for example, by replacing a hazardous adhesive with a safer one or by installing extraction equipment to control exposure to sawdust. The higher the risk, the greater the urgency to eliminate or reduce it.

The most difficult part is estimating likelihood, yet this is important if the assessment is to be meaningful, and particularly so with the more severe hazards, where the precise degree of unlikelihood may make all the difference. It is important to review risk assessments when circumstances change or if an accident or 'near miss' occurs: it may indicate that your estimation of likelihood was inaccurate.

Fire Regulations

The purpose of fire regulations is to save life, by minimizing the chance of a fire starting and by maximizing the chance of the safe evacuation of a building if one does. The materials used to build props and scenery play an important part in the latter objective by retarding the spread of flame and limiting the emission of smoke.

In the United Kingdom the usual requirement for sets and dressings upstage of a safety curtain is for materials to comply with British Standard 476: Part 7: Class 1, commonly known simply as 'Class 1'. This tests the lateral spread of flame across a vertical surface made of the material in question. Where there is no safety curtain, or for items downstage of one, there may be a requirement to meet 'Class 0'. This classification can be confusing, partly because it is not defined in BS.476, but in a number of appendices to the Building Regulations, and partly because it really applies to wall and ceiling linings only.

Materials can meet Class 0 by being non-combustible or of limited combustibility; but the most common are those that satisfy the Class 1 test and also have a low enough 'fire propagation index' as tested in BS.476 Part 6.

Fire regulations are enforced by the fire officers of the local authority licensing the venue, and the approach to unclassified materials varies from one authority to the next. Some will make small exceptions to the rules (if consulted in advance) and others will not. All will be happy to advise on what is or is not acceptable in their area and will help to solve problems if they can.

If you find that you need to treat something yourself, a wide range of flame retardants is available from theatrical suppliers. For some materials you can make your own. You need to know what the material is made of so that you can choose the right solution; the situation is particularly complex with textiles that may involve mixtures of fibres. Make sure that you get full data on and instructions for the particular product you are using; for instance, some can be diluted and others cannot. Apply according to the instructions – usually by dipping or spraying – after testing samples for effectiveness and for possible staining.

You can make your own flame retardant for wood, natural fibre fabrics, paper and straw by dissolving borax (sodium borate) and boric acid (boracic acid) in water. The exact quantities do not seem to be critical and there are many versions of the recipe, but the most common is approximately 300g borax and 250g boric acid in 5ltr water. Place the water in a stainless steel or enamelled vessel, add remaining ingredients, heat, and stir until they are dissolved. *Do not use this or any other solution not designed for the purpose for treating things worn against the skin.*

Casting and laminating materials are best treated by incorporating a suitable additive before use. There are Class 1 flame-retardant versions of some products, such as polyester resins. You can treat other materials, such as epoxy resins and latex, by mixing in the flame-retardant agent yourself; aluminium trihydrate (available as a pigment from large art materials suppliers and from chemical supply houses) and hydrated magnesium carbonate (sold as a filler in the composites industry) are the two most easily obtained and are safe to use.

WORKING WITH DRAWINGS AND REFERENCES

Sometimes designers supply a complete set of scale drawings of the props they want made, together with supporting photographic references. But, more usually, communication is less formal and more a two-way process: the designer produces a drawing or model, the maker asks for the clarification of certain details, the designer provides further drawings or references, the maker produces samples, the designer chooses from them, and so forth. Some makes are initiated on the basis of a verbal discussion alone.

Whatever the situation, it is preferable to have a drawing or reference of some sort, whether the designer or the maker produces this. It is a kind of contract, a statement of intent. It may save unnecessary work and it forms a common starting point when discussing alterations or showing the design to others. It is usually important that this includes an agreed overall size for the item; beyond this, the level of detail will vary with the item and the prevailing way of working.

Props drawings may be at 1:25 for very large pieces, but are more likely to be at 1:10 or less in scale. 'Not to scale' sketches are also useful, giving an impression of an object without the accuracy of dimensions. Additional references for details, finish or the overall 'feel' of a piece may be supplied by the designer, or found by the maker and presented to the designer for approval. The extra information such references provide helps to flesh out simple line drawings – it is hard to make something if you have no idea of what it looks like.

Also useful during the making process are life-size drawings of whatever plan, section or detail needs further clarification. Such drawings may be made on paper and used to take accurate measurements or to plan further work, or they may be drawn on plywood or hardboard and the work assembled direct on them. The degree of accuracy needed will depend on what is actually

The designer's drawings for the moose shown on p.12.

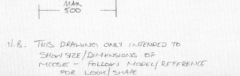

WOODEN SHIELD

ANIMATED
MOOSE

Scale 1:10 APPROX!

MAX
500

MOOSE CAN MOVE HEAD
OPEN + SHUT MOUTH
OPEN + SHUT EYES

N.B. THIS DRAWING ONLY INTENDED TO
SHOW SIZE/DIMENSIONS OF
MOOSE — FOLLOW MODEL/REFERENCE
FOR LOOK/SHAPE

BELOW: **Maker's sketch for a carved mask.**

BELOW RIGHT: **The finished mask.**

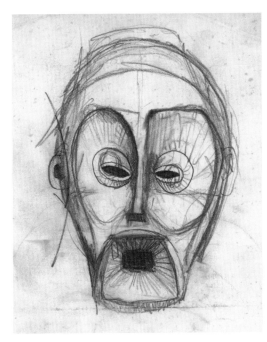

wanted from the drawing; precise drawings are the most helpful, but even rough sketches can be useful for planning and communicating.

2 WOOD

Timber on stage. The bed in this setting had eight practical drawers, although most were not used – making all of them practical allowed the blocking to change as the show developed in rehearsals. **Gianni Schicchi, GSMD;** *designer: Charlie Edwards; photograph: Laurence Burns.*

Timber is one of the prop maker's most basic resources. It is used to mimic other materials or to build structures to support them, as well as for its own appearance. It is strong, light and easy to use. Timber-based products such as plywood and MDF provide cheap, strong, sheet materials.

TIMBER TYPES

Softwood

Nearly all solid timber used on the stage is softwood. The staple softwoods of Europe are *Pinus sylvestris* and its cheaper and knottier substitute, which is a mixture of spruce and fir species. In the United Kingdom the latter are often referred to as 'white' and the pine as 'red'. Other softwoods are occasionally used, particularly when something clear (free from knots) is required: hemlock turns easily, Douglas fir is very strong and parana pine comes in very wide boards.

Hardwood

Although costly, these do still appear on stage. High-budget prop furniture makes are often hardwood, for both strength and finish: oak, beech, mahogany and meranti are all used. Turned and carved items, or any where uniformity and lack of obvious grain is desirable, may be best made from lime or jelutong. It is important when buying to ensure, first, that the wood is fully dried, as hardwood is often sold part-seasoned and, secondly, that it has come from a sustainable source. Advice on the latter can be sought from organizations such as the Forest Stewardship Council as well as from your timber merchant.

Sheet Materials

Plywood is made in a wide variety of finishes, thicknesses and grades by gluing together a number of thin layers or veneers of wood with the grain direction alternating from one layer to the next. Thus, where natural timber is strong along the grain and weak across it, plywood settles for being half as strong, but in all directions. It is usually designed for rigidity, but there are also flexible types, for forming curves; it may be obtained with decorative or plain surface veneers and with or without fire-retardant treatment. Fire regulations usually require plywood up to

(and sometimes including) 18mm in thickness to be certified as Class 1 (*see* the section on fire regulations in the first chapter). In practice, this means that all such ply is hardwood; in any case, softwood ply less than 12mm thick is mostly of poor quality. Over this thickness softwood materials designed for concrete shuttering, flooring and site hoardings, recognizable by their swirling grain and repetitive knot pattern, provide a lower budget alternative. Most plywood is not truly flat and relies on a supporting structure to make it so; if you require inherent flatness, be prepared to search – and pay – for it.

Particle boards are made by compressing particles of wood fibre with an adhesive to form sheets. The most useful to prop makers is MDF (medium density fibreboard). It is available in thicknesses from 3 up to 50mm and is fine-textured, dense and homogenous (save for a tendency to split into wafer-like layers parallel to the surface). All but the thinnest sheets are inherently flat and fire-retardant grades can be found; it carves, turns and routs easily. Thin MDF can be bent to form curves and multiple layers glued together to form laminates. It does not have the toughness of plywood, breaking suddenly when bent too far, but it does have good, local, compressive strength.

Other particle boards include hardboard (Masonite) and chipboard. Hardboard is available only in a few thicknesses; it is quite flexible, with one rough and one smooth side. Standard hardboard swells irreversibly when painted; it should be bought 'oil-tempered' to avoid this. In spite of being much cheaper than plywood of the same thickness, its main use is around the workshop, for items such as templates and mould walls.

FORMS AND SIZES

Timber

Timber can be bought 'sawn' – with a rough surface left by the saw on which it was cut – or

MDF Health and Safety

MDF has been available since the 1960s and consists of wood dust (mostly softwood) bound together with melamine/formaldehyde or urea/formaldehyde glue. The remainder is water, wax, silica and a small amount of free formaldehyde. It is classed as a softwood product. When it is machined, wood dust and formaldehyde are produced. The latter is a carcinogen, as is some hardwood dust, while softwood dust is a respiratory sensitizer (can cause occupational asthma).

Throughout the 1990s scare stories about the safety of MDF proliferated, culminating in extensive media attention. It was during this period that the myth that MDF is banned in the USA sprang up. In 1997 the Health and Safety Executive began a hazard assessment of the dangers of machining MDF. The report, published in December 1999, found it to be no more hazardous than the machining of other timber products and recommended the same control measures. Wood dust should be extracted at source wherever possible and disposable dust masks of EN149 FFP2 class or better used when necessary. Where dust extraction is not possible the use of masks is essential.

planed on one or more surfaces. Sawn timber is fine for building rough structures and for turning, but usually softwood is bought 'planed all round' or 'PAR'. Quoted timber sizes are that of the sawn timber regardless of whether it has been planed, and so planed timber is always smaller than its nominal size, usually by around 6mm on each dimension. British stock timber sizes are in millimetres, although still derived from imperial sizes in inches; the USA uses inches to describe similar stock sizes, but also expresses dimensions in units of a quarter

of an inch; for example 5/4 is the same as 1¼in. The lengths in which timber is supplied vary according to what is available to your timber merchant, and, if you need specific lengths, then you will need to say so. Common joinery sizes of pine and spruce tend to come in longer lengths than clear grades or large sections, for instance.

Mouldings

As well as coming in simple cross-sections such as rectangles and circles (dowel), both hardwood and softwood are used to make a wide variety of architectural and decorative mouldings. While some of these (such as skirting boards or parts for windows) are very specific in their use, items such as panel mouldings, architraves and stair spindles are much more versatile and a basic resource for prop making. Specialist mouldings' firms and timber merchants supplying theatre, television and film usually have the best ranges. Try to obtain charts showing the mouldings available so that designers can choose from them. A small number of suppliers also offer ready-made furniture parts such as cabriole legs; usually hardwood, these greatly speed up the production of furniture and may be cheaper than making the same thing from scratch.

Sheets

The most common size for timber-based sheet materials is 2,440mm × 1,220mm (8ft × 4ft). Note that expressed this way round, plywood will have the grain of the face veneers running along its length; 4ft × 8ft implies the grain running across the width and is less common. Larger sizes of sheet materials are available: 2,745mm × 1,220mm, 3,050mm × 1,525mm, or even 3,660mm × 1,830mm. They are less in demand and so are unlikely to work out cheaper. An oddity in the United Kingdom is 1.5mm birch ply (aircraft skin ply), which comes in 1,525mm × 1,525mm (5ft × 5ft) sheets.

RIGHT: *Using mouldings for their intended purpose – architectural decoration.*

BELOW: *Mouldings used to build up a form. A large chalice made entirely from off-the-shelf mouldings.*

BELOW RIGHT: *Common timber mouldings, all available in several sizes. Clockwise from top left: dowel, half round, quadrant, ogee architrave, chair rail, ogee panel moulding, scotia, astragal and a bullnose-and-scotia nosing.*

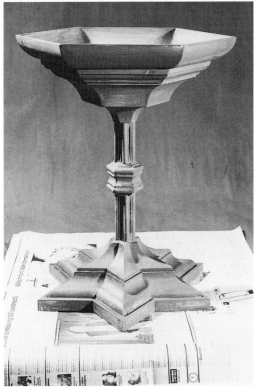

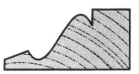

Woodworking Tools

Basic Tools
tape measure
try-square or combination square
sliding bevel gauge
trammel heads or large compasses
block plane or jack plane
round and flat rasps
mallet and chisels
hammer
utility panel saw
mitre box
clamps and vice
ratchet screwdriver or
   cordless driver/drill

electric jigsaw
power drill, drill bits and countersinking bit

Advanced Tools
hand-held circular saw
belt sander
plunge router
pneumatic stapler and nail gun and a small
   air compressor to power them
band saw
lathe
pillar drill
crosscut and bench saws
mortising and tenoning machines

MEASURING AND MARKING OUT

Decide on the level of accuracy you need. Some work – a mechanism with moving parts, for instance – may require very precise measurement, while you may be able to set other things out by eye. For fine work mark the wood with a sharp, hard pencil – 2H is ideal – or a knife. Remove marks with medium sandpaper rather than an eraser. In some machine operations, such as ripping timber to width on a bench or bandsaw, no mark is necessary on the stock itself – the fence is simply set the required distance from the blade and the work fed through. When cutting multiples of the same length on a crosscut saw only the first need be marked up; a stop can then be clamped to the fence against the end of this and subsequent pieces slid up to this to repeat the same length. Use a try-square to mark across timber or ply or to test the squareness of small joints or corners. Check the squareness of larger structures by comparing the length of the diagonals, or use a large, home-made, wooden square that you know is accurate.

A bevel gauge or 'sliding bevel' can be set to different angles and used for marking and checking and for setting up angles on machines. Bisect angles by drawing two lines parallel to those that form the angle and a third through their intersection to the corner.

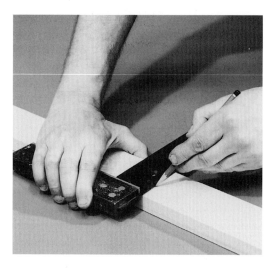

Using a try-square.

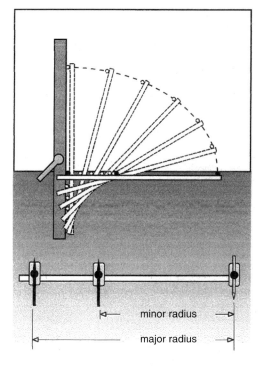

minor radius

major radius

ABOVE: Using three trammel heads to draw a quarter ellipse. One pin runs up a straightedge clamped to the board, and the other along the edge of the board itself.

RIGHT: Bisecting an angle using parallel lines, and using a bevel gauge to transfer the angle to a moulding.

BELOW: Using trammel heads to draw an arc.

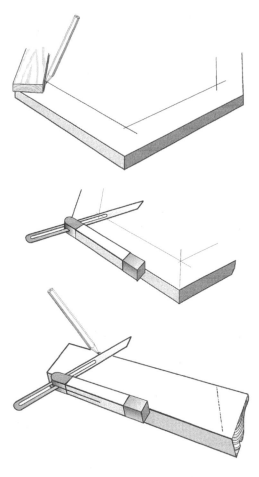

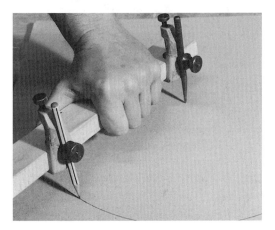

Use a marking gauge to scribe a line parallel to an edge, or a combination square with a pencil held against its end. To mark in or out from a curved edge, use a washer or carefully cut disc of card; place the pencil in the middle and roll the disc along a strip of card held against the edge.

To mark out circles use trammel heads on a length of wood, or just knock two nails through it. To draw an ellipse, use two nails and a piece of string – be prepared for the result to be a bit rough. For greater accuracy, use three trammel heads and a wooden straightedge, as illustrated, to draw a quarter ellipse, then cut this out and use it as a template.

Long, shallow arcs and curves that are not part of a circle can be marked out by drawing along a 'spline'; this is a slender length of wood, metal or flexible material bent to the points you want the curve to pass through. This enables you to draw complex or non-geometric curves quickly, though you may need several pairs of hands.

CUTTING AND SHAPING WOOD

In theory, all you need to cut wood is a handsaw or two, but your progress will be painfully slow.

Most people will soon wish to invest in something that plugs into the wall. The familiar electric jigsaw is an extremely versatile tool and, although not quite a precision instrument, is capable of work of great intricacy with some practice. Its complement is the hand-held circular saw, which cuts straight lines straighter and faster; in its smaller forms it may also be used for cutting timber to length. Both these tools offer great portability and versatility.

Machines – tools to which the wood is brought – mostly perform more specific tasks and do them better. A cross-cut or radial arm saw can be used to cut timber to length and to cut mitres (angles) and certain joints. A bench saw, or circular saw

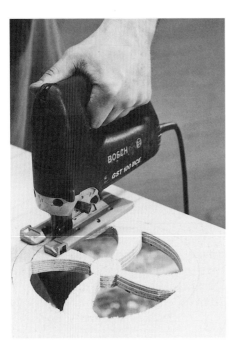

*ABOVE: **Using a jigsaw.***

Using a band saw. The table has been tilted to 45 degrees to make square stock octagonal before rounding with a plane.

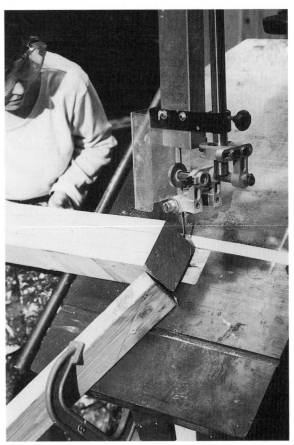

bench, is used for ripping timber to width, cutting bevels and splays, and for cutting up sheet materials. Both may be used for more complex tasks with the aid of jigs and fixtures. Wall saws offer fast and accurate rectangular cutting of sheet materials (but little else), without taking up much floor space.

By far the most versatile machine, from the prop maker's point of view, is the band saw. The huge variety of blades available makes possible all kinds of straight and curved cutting. The table tilts for angled cuts and splays; simple jigs facilitate tasks such as disc-cutting and pattern-following; furniture parts can be produced quickly. It can also be used to cut plastics, expanded polystyrene, upholstery foam and much more.

Hand tools for shaping wood include rasps (which continue to be useful for smoothing and refining the shape of furniture parts cut on the band saw) and chisels and gouges for carving. Even with much practice woodcarving remains a slow process that does not fit easily into modern work schedules, and is likely to be replaced by a modelling and casting process. Two power tools much more likely to be in everyday use are small, hand-held belt sanders and routers. The former are invaluable for fast smoothing, rounding or general 'tidying'; the latter are versatile machining and moulding tools. Both can remove material very quickly and therefore produce a lot of waste. Goggles and a dust mask are essential and, if possible, extraction at source as well.

ABOVE: A belt sander in use on a furniture carcass.

Using a router to cut a circular moulding – in this case part of a clock face.

Woodwork Health and Safety

- *Working with wood is dangerous.* Always ensure that you are familiar with and confident about the safe use of tools and machinery. If you are not sure about the safety of something, do not do it; seek advice from a competent person.
- *Protect your hands.* Always ensure that the appropriate machine guards are in place. Use push-sticks whenever possible. When using chisels and gouges always cut away from your body and from your free hand. Wear gloves when handling large pieces of sawn timber and sheets of plywood.
- *Protect your eyes and ears.* Wear goggles whenever you use power tools or machinery; get into the habit of wearing them at all times. Ear defenders are necessary with many electric tools and machines.
- *Protect your lungs.* Breathing in softwood dust may cause occupational asthma, while some hardwood dusts are carcinogenic. Use dust-extraction equipment whenever possible. Many small power tools, such as routers and jigsaws, are now designed to be hooked up to dust extractors. Wear a disposable FFP2 dust mask as well for very dusty work, or whenever extraction is not available. Make sure that it fits properly, is kept clean and is stored in a clean bag when not in use, and is thrown away after the recommended time – usually 8hr of use.
- *Protect yourself from electric shock.* Check plugs and leads regularly for damage and replace them when necessary. Ensure that plugs are fitted with the right fuse for each tool and, if possible, have sockets fitted with RCD protection. Do not run extension leads where they may be damaged by tools or materials.
- *Protect yourself from falls.* Keep your work area tidy; clear away offcuts regularly. Do not leave tools, materials or extension leads where they may create a trip hazard.
- *Protect others.* Consider the safety of others as much as your own; all the above points apply to them too.

JOINING WOOD AND WOOD PRODUCTS

There are many ways to join wood; the choice depends on how strong and how neat the joint must be. In general, the more strength is required, the more time, skill or equipment will be needed. Joining techniques divide into two groups: traditional carpenters' joints, where one or both pieces are shaped to provide a good mechanical join and/or considerable contact area for glue, are strong but time-consuming to make; the best known is probably the mortise and tenon joint. Lap and butt joints, where the parts are simply overlapped or butted together, rely on fastenings such as nails or screws as well as glue. They are quicker to make and, while rarely as strong as traditional joints, are often quite adequate. Other types of butt joint can be made with glue alone – examples are laminated curves (*see* the section on making curved surfaces below) and small decorative constructions.

Using Nails and Screws

For most construction work butt or lap joints using glue and metal fasteners are good enough and much faster to make. Nails are cheap and fast but require a solid support against which to hammer. They may work loose if repeatedly stressed, but are useful where the stress is known to be lim-

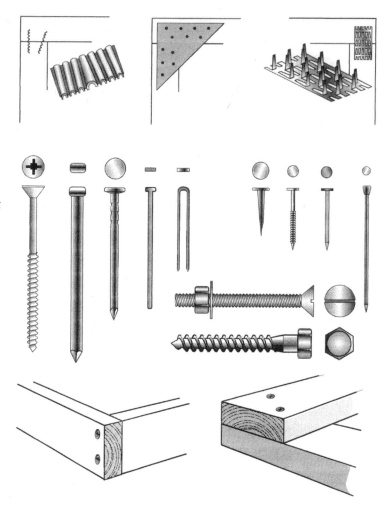

Timber framing. Top: corner joints in flat stock, using corrugated fasteners, nailed plywood plate and timber connector.

Middle: fastenings. Clockwise from left: screw, oval nail, round wire nail, pneumatic brad, pneumatic staple, bayonet tack, ring-shank nail, cement-coated nail, panel pin, coach screw and machine screw with nut and washer.

Bottom: using woodscrews to make butt joints.

ited, as in fixing decoration on to something, or in carefully designed or braced structures. Ring-shank or cement-coated nails can both be used in situations requiring more grip, such as fixing thin plywood around curves. Panel pins are useful for jobs such as attaching mouldings. Delicate parts split less often if you nip or file the sharp point off the pin.

Screws pull the two parts of a joint together tightly and are unlikely to work loose; they may also be used where work is not firmly supported.

Old-fashioned, tapered screws needed carefully drilled pilot holes to allow the wedge-like action of thread and head to force the joint together. Modern, parallel-sided screws, at least when used in softwood, are easier to use, needing only a thin or shallow pilot hole and a countersink; they also hold effectively in end-grain. They are sized by length and by thickness, the latter expressed in 'numbers' (No.8, No.10: the smaller the number, the thinner the screw), or in metric conversions of these (for example, 4.2, 5.3).

At least half or two-thirds of the length of the screw should be in the piece of wood being screwed into. For putting screws in, the cordless electric screwdriver is now ubiquitous, although pump-action, ratchet screwdrivers are almost as fast. Manual screwdrivers are best reserved for delicate tasks (and for opening tins of paint).

Pneumatic staple or nail guns, run from air compressors, do the work of pins and nails very quickly, whether it is applying mouldings or cladding frames with thin plywood. Large, lightweight forms can be built up tea-chest style with 20mm × 20mm timber and 4mm ply. Solid support is not necessary – the staples are fired so fast that the wood has no time to react.

Wood Glues

The most common and convenient wood glue is the white, water-based PVA available in every hardware shop. The more expensive brands dry harder and are more waterproof; often cheaper glue will do, since hardness is only important in items such as furniture and in laminating curved surfaces; you may well choose something stronger for these tasks in any case.

Stronger and faster, but just as easy to use, is aliphatic resin ('yellow glue'), sold mostly in model shops. It sets hard enough to be sanded away, producing fewer visible glue lines than PVA.

Pearl glue, a form of animal glue, is still useful as a cheap, strong and hard glue for furniture, laminating or veneering. It needs to be freshly made: soak in water overnight, pour off surplus water and melt in a double boiler or electric gluepot. The open time (the time before the glue gels, during which the parts need to be brought together) is very short. The glue is also not waterproof, being soluble in hot water; this might be considered an advantage since no other common adhesive is reversible. Adding urea inhibits gelling and greatly increases the working time, but probably affects the strength; adding formalin (formaldehyde solution) makes the glue insoluble in water after drying.

Epoxy resin is the most important high-strength adhesive. Changing from syrupy liquid to hard, resilient solid on mixing with a hardener, it can be modified by adding fillers, thickeners, solvents or reinforcement to produce high-strength, gap-filling adhesives in a variety of consistencies and setting times. Quantities available vary from twin tubes of 'five-minute epoxy' for small-scale work to bulk packs with pumps to deliver the correct ratio of resin to hardener. The significant drawbacks are high price and the need to avoid all skin contact with both the resin and the hardener. The enormous potential of epoxy lies in its inherent structural strength, giving it unequalled gap-filling properties and enabling butt joints to be made without mechanical fastenings such as screws or pins. This, in turn, opens up new possibilities for lightweight construction, where, for example, a fillet of thickened epoxy may replace a wooden batten, or a butt joint may be made without the need to drill through delicate parts.

Furniture

Although much stage furniture is hired, bought or borrowed, it is also made from scratch if that is more economical or if the design requires it. How much of an undertaking it is depends on the item (chairs, for instance, tend to be more difficult to make than tables) and its style (rustic benches being much quicker to construct and finish than elegant dining chairs). The question of finish is important with high-class period furniture: even though stage furniture is unlikely to need to match the real thing in finesse, finishing it can be as time-consuming as constructing it.

Another deciding factor will be the shaping equipment (and expertise) that a particular design demands. While a simple bench may need only a few hand tools and perhaps a router, more

Chaise longue adapted for the GSMD production of Krenek's **Der Diktator;** *designer: Isabella Bywater; photograph: Laurence Burns.*

elaborate projects are likely to call for a band saw or lathe and accompanying dust extraction. An important alternative for those with limited equipment or time is to buy hard-to-make components such as turned or cabriole legs.

Materials

The presence of knots in standard softwood grades indicates unreliable strength; you need to assess its suitability on the basis of the design. How slender are the parts? Is it inherently strong, or does it rely on the strength of a particular component? Check the intended use of the item as well: will a male opera singer be standing on it to sing an aria, or just putting his hat down on it?

Knots also cut down the options for finishing because they are likely to need to be hidden with an opaque primer, although anything that is constructed from a mixture of materials will probably need this anyway.

To avoid knots, you can either carefully select suitable pieces from your normal timber or buy clear stock for the job. Clear softwoods in large pieces can cost as much as some hardwoods and the latter are usually a better choice.

MDF, blockboard and ply are all useful sheet materials. MDF routs and carves well and shows cleaner edges than either ply or blockboard. It is flatter than plywood of comparable price. Most blockboard is lighter than ply or MDF and it can be bought with a variety of surface veneers.

Mortise and Tenon Joints

These are all but indispensable for high-stress joints such as those between the legs and rails of chairs or tables. If you want to make this kind of furniture, it is important to have a way of cutting the two parts of this joint. Many scenic construction workshops have mortise and tenon cutting machines and, if you have access to these, you will not have many problems in cutting these joints. If not, there are a number of other ways. The most obvious is to cut them by hand in the traditional manner – the tools needed are few and the techniques straightforward. Consistent results demand practice and even then the method remains quite slow, so it is one suited only to those with time on their hands.

Tenons can be cut with a variety of power tools: a band saw, a cross-cut saw with either a

31

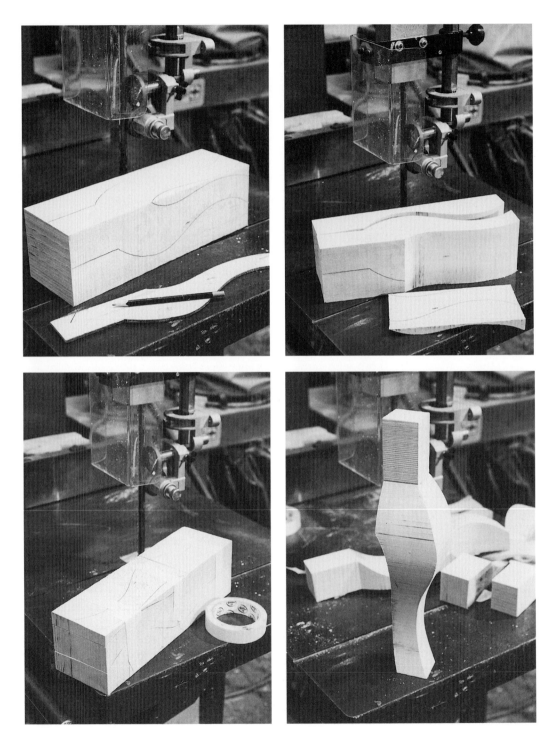

OPPOSITE PAGE:

TOP LEFT: *Cutting a cabriole leg on a band saw – a classic example of the technique of producing three-dimensional parts for furniture. The profile of the leg is first drawn on to two adjacent sides of the stock.*
TOP RIGHT: *One profile is cut out, and the offcuts saved.*
BOTTOM LEFT: *The offcuts are taped back in place and the second profile is cut.*
BOTTOM RIGHT: *The resulting leg, ready for sanding.*

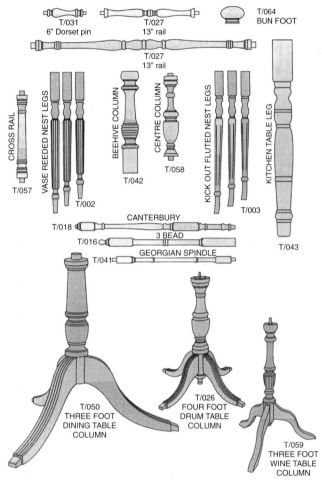

ABOVE: *Part of the selection of ready-made furniture parts offered by one London manufacturer. Courtesy: D. & J. Simons.*

LEFT: *Injection-moulded plastic mouldings used to simulate wood carving on picture frames.*

normal blade raised or a dado cutter, or a bench saw will all produce consistent tenons (although, unlike those made on a tenoning machine, their thickness will vary with that of the stock). Designs for home-made router jigs for tenon cutting can be found in DIY woodworking literature.

There are fewer ways to cut mortices: hollow-chisel kits are available to fit some pillar drills, or router jigs can be bought or made. Drilling a row of holes and then using a manual mortising chisel is possible when all you are cutting is eight joints for a table or stool.

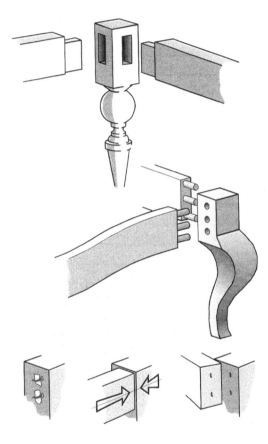

Two ways to join chair legs. The mortise and tenon (top) is stronger, but slower to make without machines. Dowel joints (below) are strong if used with a high-strength adhesive. Mark hole centres by taping a small tack to one side of the joint and pressing the pieces together. The drill can be aligned by eye or with an inexpensive jig.

Dowel joints, which are butt joints reinforced with glued pegs of dowelling, can replace mortice and tenon joints in situations where less stress is expected, or when they are used with strong glues such as epoxies (although the uses to which something may be put on stage are not always predictable).

Mending and Reinforcing Furniture

There are two kinds of repair to old or broken furniture which may be required: temporary structural measures to keep something going for a few more shows, and careful restoration of both strength and appearance. Reinforcement is usually to prevent damage in strenuous action. All three are easier if the furniture is yours, not something hired or borrowed.

Temporary structural repairs are carried out because part of the furniture has broken or started to break, or a joint has become loose. The usual approach to broken parts is to attach a piece of wood or a metal bracket to take the strain, like a splint. The point of these repairs is to stop the damage from getting worse, not return the item to its original strength. The stronger they are, the more ugly they are likely to be. Loose joints are best solved with fresh glue, if you can get enough of it in there; otherwise some kind of steel strap or bracket may be used to hold the two parts of the joint together. Where a round tenon or rail-end has worked loose in its socket in a chair leg, resist the temptation to screw through from the other side of the leg into the endgrain of the rail – the screw will not stay tight for long and the leg is weakened.

A restoration-type of repair is often time-consuming even if the damage that prompts it is limited; replacing a single broken rail, for example, may mean the dismantling of several other joints. The glue in old joints often perishes and traditional hide glue can be softened by steaming; but small steel brads or pins will probably have been used to hold the joint together as it dried. Damage inflicted in extracting these entails further repair. Where a part has split, it may be possible to glue it back together, otherwise, a copy must be made. Try to use similar coloured timber to simplify refinishing; copy the dimensions of the old part carefully. It may not be necessary to reproduce the exact shape or level of detail; the main point is that the new part does not draw attention to

A prototype chair made in a few hours by a group of students. The joinery of stage furniture may be quicker than the finishing of it.

BELOW: *MDF carves easily and crisply with hand tools.*

BOTTOM: *A carcass made of cheap softwood. After upholstery, only the legs and the fronts of the arms will be visible.*

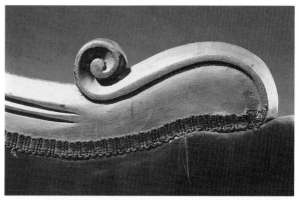

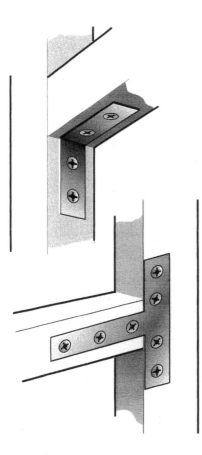

Emergency furniture repairs using metal brackets. Such repairs are never as strong as the original joint.

furniture was already weak through old age or previous damage, then it was ill-chosen, but at least the problem can probably be solved by careful repair. If, however, the piece was sound and the damage was caused entirely by the way it was used, then, however well you mend it, it is likely to happen again. This is important because it may have implications for the performers' safety and because there is likely to be pressure to get the item back on stage or into rehearsal quickly. What is needed in this situation is not just repair, but reinforcement, based on an understanding of what will happen to the furniture on stage and of the stresses this will place on it. Solutions may vary from remaking joints with epoxy glue and reinforcing around them with fillets of epoxy and chopped glass, to fabricating bespoke brackets in heavy gauge steel.

FURNITURE ON RAKED STAGES

A rake is a sloping floor: either the whole stage (many older theatres have a slight gradient because it helped reduce the total height of the building) or as part of a set.

If you put an ordinary table on a rake, its legs will no longer be vertical and its top will be at the same angle as the rake. With the very slight gradients of whole-stage architectural rakes this rarely matters and adjusting the table to give a truly horizontal top merely draws unwanted attention to the rake. But, with the steeper slopes of rakes that are used as design elements, such adjustment becomes more common and is known as 'anti-raking'.

Rake Geometry

Before you can build or modify a piece of furniture for a rake, you need two crucial pieces of information:

* The slope of the rake (also simply known as 'the rake'). This is the angle between the plane of the rake and a horizontal plane and

itself. When reassembling furniture you must decide whether to use epoxy, which is very strong and convenient but prevents the need for future dismantling, or hide glue.

The structure of chairs in particular (and most of what needs to be mended seems to be chairs) is such that, when one joint goes, extra stress is put on those around it, and they soon follow. This is particularly so when the cause of failure is some unusual or extreme use of the item in performance, for example in a fight or dance sequence. If the root cause was that the can be expressed in one of three ways, in degrees, as a ratio or as a percentage; for example, 7.125 degrees, 1:8 (one in eight) and 12.5 per cent all describe the same slope. Degrees are the most accurate method and lead straight into trigonometry if you need to make detailed calculations about the rake. Ratios are the traditional form of expression; they are easily visualized and useful for discussions with people less interested in mathematics. What they mean is that, in this instance, the slope goes up one unit for every eight travelled along the floor and they convert easily into angles for trigonometry (the reciprocal of the second number is the tangent of the angle of rake). Percentages are the least often used and are just another way of giving a ratio – divide by 100 to get the tangent of the angle.

✳ You must also know how the piece of furniture will be set in relation to the way the rake slopes. Suppose a rectangular table is anti-raked so as to be level when set with its length running up and down the rake. Turn it 90 degrees and the top will be at a crazy angle; turn it another 90 and it will slope down at twice the angle of the rake. The only position in which the top will be level is the one it was originally anti-raked for. If the piece in question is important in the action, the director (quite reasonably) may not wish to be tied down to a particular position and it will be best to leave the anti-raking as late as possible; a piece being made from scratch

can be made with four equal legs and later modified.

Note that the direction in which a designer's rake slopes (the direction of steepest slope, or 'way' of the rake) is not necessarily going to be straight up and down stage. Neither need it be parallel with the sides of the rake nor square to the front or back; this is the case in rakes whose front edge is a long, tapering step. This is what people usually mean when they use the term 'double rake' or similar expressions.

For the purposes of anti-raking furniture, the all-important factors are the direction of steepest slope and the orientation of the piece relative to that direction. Often, whoever is building the rake itself has done a lot of work on its geometry and may be able to tell you all you need. If not, you will have to work it out for yourself. In plan, the direction of steepest slope is at right angles to any line drawn through two points of equal height; so, as long as you have two such points – two high points, a line where the rake meets the stage or whatever – then things are relatively straightforward.

Anti-Raking Tables and Chairs
With plain-legged furniture, by far the easiest way to anti-rake is to cut the right amount off each leg. Adding to legs is more difficult, especially when there is likely to be a dynamic load, as with chairs, but it can be done. Turned or cabriole legs do not anti-rake easily and the only solution may be to make legs of different lengths from scratch. Trimming or extending the legs of hired or borrowed furniture is rarely possible. Work out how much to remove from each leg in the following way, by using either the piece itself or a scale drawing.

1. Either on your scale drawing or on the floor, draw a line showing the direction of slope and at right angles to it a base line: a line connecting points of equal height.

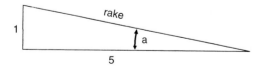

Ways of expressing slope. This rake could be described as: one in five, 20 per cent or 11.3 degrees.

2. Position the furniture or indicate its legs on the drawing, so that the most 'downhill' leg is on the base line and the piece is at the intended angle to the direction of slope.

3. Measure the shortest distance from each leg to the base line; this will be along a line at right angles to the base line.

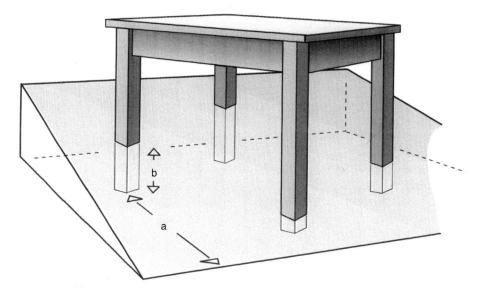

ABOVE: Anti-raking a table. Knowing the rake and the distance along the floor to each leg from a base line (a) enables you to calculate how much to cut off (b) or extend it by.

BELOW: Extending a leg. 1: find a piece of steel tube of similar diameter to the bottom of the leg; calculate the extension needed, add 30 per cent for fixing it on and deducting a bit for a plug if necessary; cut and clean up the ends inside and out. 2: carefully carve away the bottom of the leg until the tube will fit tightly on to it. 3: tap on the tube with an old mallet. 4: carve or turn a wooden plug to prevent floor damage.

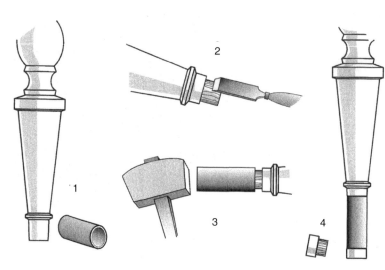

4. Multiply each of these measurements by the tangent of the rake angle or divide by the second number in the ratio to find out how much to remove from each leg. It is the distance between the bottoms of the legs that matters, not the overall size of a tabletop, for instance.

MAKING CURVED SURFACES

From jewellery boxes to rowing boats, many props call for curved wooden surfaces. There are several techniques by which to make them.

* *Cutting from solid timber.* Furniture parts such as crest rails for chair backs are traditionally made in this way; the requirements are a piece of wood big enough to yield the desired shape and a suitable tool – probably a band saw, jigsaw or router – to cut it with. Often a 'blank' big enough for the piece can be made by gluing up two or more pieces of wood.

* *Stressed skin.* A common scenic construction technique suitable for both small and very large curved surfaces. A thin, flexible sheet material is fixed over a series of 'formers' cut to the required curve. The skin may be plywood (1.5mm birch or gaboon, or 4mm birch for greater strength), hardboard or thin MDF. Formers are typically made of 18 or 25mm ply or solid timber. Some stress remains in the skin and it is best to fix it with both glue and tightly gripping fasteners, such as cement-coated or ring shank nails. Unless extreme, this stress should not cause distortion since the formers are so much stronger.

* *Laminating.* If several thin layers of timber are glued together on a jig that holds them in the desired curve, the resulting 'lamination' will retain that shape (or one close to it) when the glue dries. If it is tightly clamped while gluing and soft, creeping glue such as cheap PVA is avoided, its strength should be similar to a piece of solid timber of the same thickness. A certain amount of spring-back is inevitable, but the thinner the layers and the more of them there are, the less it will be. Laminating may be as simple as sticking two layers of 4mm ply together in a slight curve to make a chair back, which is a fairly quick job. The more complex the task, the more time-consuming it is likely to be to prepare multiple layers of timber and design and build a jig. Quicker alternatives should be explored first. One variation that is much faster than true laminating is 'staving', where a core of wooden battens is sandwiched between two skins of thin timber or sheet material. The result is very strong with little spring-back.

* *Kerfing.* This involves making a series of parallel saw cuts nearly all the way through the wood, filling them with glue and then bending the wood to the desired curve so that the saw cuts close up. For extra strength, a thin skin may then be applied to the concave side. Trial and error or calculation may be required to

Bending skin ply over a curve. A piece of 1.5mm gaboon ply being fixed to two MDF formers – the ends of a box – with air staples.

Curves cut from solid wood.

BELOW: Laminating three pieces of 9mm timber on to a former cut from an old scaffolding board. The wedges help to fair the curve where there are irregularities in the former.

find the number, depth and spacing of the saw cuts. This technique is difficult without a radial arm saw since equal depth and spacing are crucial. It is possible to buy MDF with pre-cut kerfs along or across the length of the sheet – ask your timber merchant.

Cut-from-solid or stressed-skin techniques are the fastest and most common. Laminating or kerfing should be reserved for situations when they are more appropriate, such as when greater strength is needed or there is not room for formers.

TURNING

The ability to turn wood is important for furniture making, and for countless other items from chandeliers to porridge bowls. The principle is simple and ancient: a piece of wood is fixed to the lathe spindle and made to rotate. A cutting tool, firmly supported by a tool rest fixed to the lathe bed, is then placed in the path of the moving wood; the turner manipulates the tool to remove material to produce the desired shape.

The basic techniques may be acquired with a reasonable amount of practice. There seems to be some snobbery surrounding woodturning

and it is easy to be put off by, for instance, the idea that the use of sandpaper or scraping tools is not 'proper' turning. Practising turners know that these are as much a part of the toolkit as anything else; in any case, the highly-polished finish achieved by craftsman turners is rarely required on the stage and, if the work is to be painted, is not as good as a sanded finish.

Timber for Turning

Both carcassing and joinery grades of softwood can be frustrating to turn because of the number of knots and the great variations in hardness between the early wood (lighter parts of the grain) and the late wood (dark). The weakness of the early wood means that damage may be extensive if a tool catches, and fine details are

ABOVE: Part of a candlestick being turned on the lathe.

vulnerable. Nevertheless, they are fine for a lot of work. The alternatives are all more expensive. Better quality pines as well as clear hemlock and Douglas fir are all available in large sections. Among hardwoods, oak, beech and mahogany turn well. Jelutong is light, cuts easily and is very useful when its lower strength is not an issue.

A frequent problem is the price of solid timber big enough for large work, and a common solution is to glue together pieces of smaller section. It is obviously important that the pieces are well joined, since the stresses involved in roughing are high and the consequences of a laminated blank breaking up at 600rpm could be serious. The following measures will help to ensure strength:

* Make sure that surfaces to be joined fit closely. If they do not, use a gap-filling adhesive such as epoxy resin.
* Spread glue generously and evenly and apply pressure with a vice, clamps or weights while it sets.
* Allow plenty of time for the glue to cure – 24 hours for epoxy, 48 for PVA.

Cracks often appear in laminated work a while after it is been turned owing to the movement of the separate pieces relative to one another. This

A laminated or 'brick-laid' blank for a bowl.

process is exacerbated by the moisture in PVA glue and by using wood straight from the timber merchant. Usually such cracks can just be filled, but, if they would be a problem, use timber that has already adjusted to the moisture level in your workshop and stick it together with epoxy. Blanks for bowls may be built up by a process of 'bricklaying' small pieces of wood on a circular base. It is usually necessary to make a life-size drawing to work out the numbers and sizes of the pieces in each layer. The more layers and pieces there are, the more tolerance should be allowed for errors in centring the work as it is built up and when it is mounted on the lathe.

Equipment

A lathe for props work should ideally have a wide range of speeds, from around 300rpm for roughing large work, up to 2,000 for turning slender spindles. It should be as heavy and rigid as possible (vibration is the enemy of good turning) and needs a centre height of 100mm and around 800mm between centres if it is to accommodate a large table leg. Greater centre height would be useful and a means to work 'outboard' allows you to turn wide objects such as bowls from a face-plate. Although mechanically straightforward, large lathes are expensive because they are very heavy. If you are limited to a light bench-top lathe, bolt it securely to the heaviest workbench you have and do not push it beyond its limits (it will soon let you know if you do).

The nominal centre height may be reduced in practice by the way the tool rest is mounted. Most tool rests are quite short; frequent repositioning is necessary and features such as long tapers can be awkward to cut. An optional, long tool rest may be available, or you can make one if you have steel fabrication equipment. Fixed-height tool rests should be at centre height, although a few centimetres adjustment to either side is better.

Headstock chucks are not standard equipment on wood lathes, but are a useful extra for

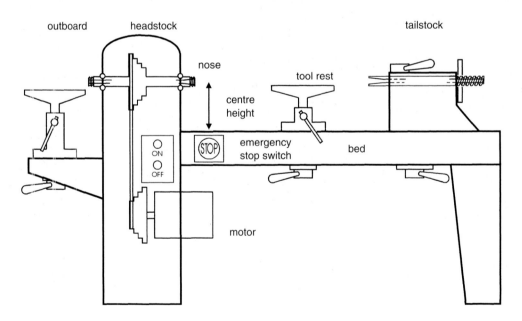

The parts of a typical medium-sized wood lathe.

holding work too small or delicate for faceplate or centres. There are several combination chucks specifically for woodturning on the market, but they are expensive; an alternative for bigger lathes is to look for used metal lathe chucks to fit your spindle nose thread. Three-jaw, self-centring chucks hold stock that is already round, while four-jaw independent chucks hold rectangular stock, off-centre if necessary. Firms supplying used lathes for model engineering can supply these. Such chucks may have projecting parts and should be properly guarded.

A tailstock chuck fits in the taper bore of the tailstock spindle and is used to hold drill bits for drilling down the central axis of the work. It is the same kind of three-jaw chuck as is found on large, hand-held, power drills, but with a taper shank mounting; it is not nearly as expensive as a headstock chuck and, like all turning equipment, may be found second-hand.

Tools

The cutting tools used to shape the work are very important. You do not need many, but they should be heavy and have handles up to twice as long as the blades. A good turning tool balances at the point where the blade enters the handle, or just on to the handle. Do not buy sets of cheap, undersized tools; buy a few good ones.

Turning tools divide into those that remove wood by scraping it off (scrapers) and those that use a paring or slicing action (chisels and gouges). Often you can choose between tools of one or the other type to perform a given task; a few tools work in both ways. There are four important 'slicing' tools:

* *Roughing gouge.* Used to turn square stock down to a cylinder and for very rough shaping. It usually has a large, heavy, deeply U-shaped blade.

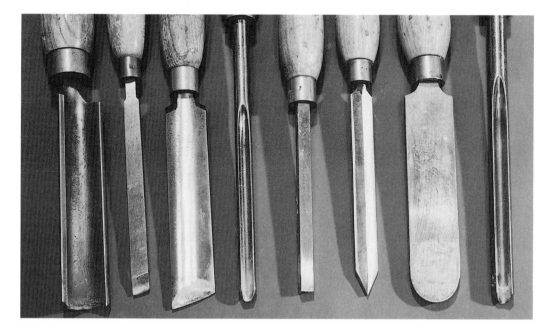

Woodturning tools. Left to right: roughing gouge, two skew chisels, fingernail gouge, bedan, parting tool, round-nosed scraper and bowl gouge.

* *Skew chisel.* Probably the turner's most important tool; it is used like plane, for shaping cylindrical, tapered, convex or shallowly-concave forms. It also functions as a knife for cutting into work and facing off ends. The cutting edge is at around 60 degrees to the axis of the tool; the cross-section is rectangular or oval. The blade is ground to a shallow bevel on both sides of the cutting edge; there is usually about 20 degrees between the bevels. Turning tools have no secondary bevel (unlike joinery chisels) and the whole of each bevel is stoned each time they are sharpened.
* *Fingernail gouge.* A long, relatively narrow gouge, with its bevel ground quite shallow in the middle, but progressively steeper round the sides. This gives it the shape that suggests its name. It is used when turning between centres for cutting deep coves (concave forms). It can also do most of what a skew chisel does, although not always as cleanly. It may be seen as a skew with its corners curved sharply up out of the way.
* *Bowl gouge.* A shorter, stockier gouge with a steep bevel ground square across the end. Used for shaping the outsides of bowls and other large diameter work. Of little use in spindle turning.

Chisels and gouges cut with the handle lower than the blade, which cuts on the upper half of the work. But scraping tools are used with the blade pointing downwards and removing material from just below the centreline. The cutting face is all but square to the top of the tool and the edge itself is a minute steel burr raised by sharpening on a bench grinder. The most important of these tools are:

* *Round-nosed scraper.* Wide blade with the front ground to a sweeping curve, used to cut coves, even out concave surfaces, or plane knots.

* *Square scraper.* Used for facing bottoms of hollows, forming spigots and evening out convex forms.
* *Form tools.* The cutting edges of these are ground to the profile of a particular feature such as a small bead. They help to achieve uniformity in production turning and can be reground to suit a particular task.

Two common tools can be used both as chisels and as scrapers:

* *Parting tool.* Thin-bladed tool used to cut deep, narrow slots into work early in the shaping process and to sever it from the stock when finished. The blade's cross-section tapers away from the line of the cutting edge to reduce friction.
* *Bedan.* Square-sectioned blade with a steep bevel on the end; used to cut slots and turn spigots and as a chisel to form small details such as beads.

Mounting Work in the Lathe

Long, thin work such as legs or spindles is turned 'between centres' – driven by a toothed spur at the headstock end and supported by a conical tailstock centre. Work is prepared by punching the centres at each end. The drive spur can be made to bite by making shallow saw cuts across the end of the work, or by removing the spur from the machine and using it as a punch (with a short length of steel tube used to protect the taper). The tailstock is positioned to give a little clearance with the centre retracted, and locked down. The work is held in place and the centre is brought up under pressure against it with the quill and locked off. Tailstock centres are either 'live' (revolve with the work) or 'dead' (do not); the latter may need to be lubricated or tightened during the work. Both types may need to be tightened if there is a catch or impact during the roughing process; slip a washer or a copper coin with a

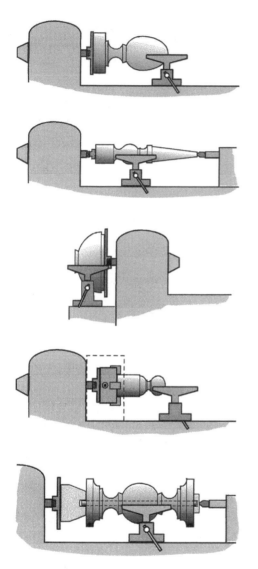

Different ways to hold work in the lathe. From top: on a faceplate, between centres, on an outboard faceplate, in a chuck and on a mandrel. The last ensures that turning is concentric around a bore. A steel tube that fits the bore locates in holes in the large block on the faceplate and the small one on the tailstock centre. Pressure from the tailstock grips the stock between centres.

hole drilled in it over the tailstock centre to apply pressure without the centre burying itself in the end of the work.

Where work turned between centres needs a hole right down the middle of it, there are several solutions. If the hole is narrow (say for wiring up a lamp) it can be drilled with a 'long boring tool', provided that the tailstock quill is bored through. The usual tailstock centre is exchanged for a ring centre and the boring tool – essentially a long auger bit – is passed through the tailstock to cut down the middle of the work.

Larger bores are best made in the stock before the work is turned, either by drilling or by laminating the stock to leave a central void. The work can then be mounted in the lathe either by inserting a well-fitting plug into each end of the stock and using the normal centres, or by using a mandrel set-up (*see* diagram).

When it is impracticable to turn work between centres, it is either held in a chuck or mounted on a faceplate. The former suits small work such as finials and can be a three- or four-jaw chuck of the metal-turning type, a collet chuck designed for woodturning, or an improvised wooden arrangement (*see* diagram). There is also what is known as a screw chuck, which is actually more like a small faceplate with a single, large screw in the centre. Faceplates screw on to the threaded nose of the lathe and have a selection of screw holes by which work can be attached to them. They may also be used to mount blocks of wood for turning improvised chucks and jigs.

Shaping Techniques

Most between-centres work proceeds in the same basic order. First, the work is turned from square to cylindrical section. Then a series of slots is cut in strategic places to measured depths. These act as reference points for the main shaping work. Next, any fine detail is added and the work is sanded if necessary.

Lastly, it may need to be parted off from a larger piece of stock held in the lathe.

Roughing

The tool rest is positioned as close as possible without fouling and at centre height. (Every time the tool rest is moved, the work should be turned by hand to ensure that it clears.) Set the lathe on its lowest speed and switch it on. Place the roughing gouge on the tool rest at one end of the work, with the blade square to the work and the handle horizontal. Hold it with one hand (usually the right if you are right-handed) on the handle and the other holding the blade, but also bearing against the tool rest. Point the tool slightly in the direction you are

Cutting a pommel with a skew chisel.

Roughing. The gouge is moving from right to left.

going to go; roll it so that its top surface inclines slightly in that direction and drop the handle so that the blade points slightly upwards. The effect of these three small angles is to present part of the bevel of the gouge at a tangent to the circle through which the wood is moving so that it cuts with a slicing action; experiment with these angles to find the combination that cuts best.

Move the gouge in to meet the revolving wood. At first you will just be cutting off the corners and it is easier to hear or feel than to see them – they are part of the transparent blur around the edges of the moving wood. When you feel the gouge cutting the corners, move it steadily along the length of the work. When you reach the other end, reverse the angles and come back the other way (it is important to be able to do everything in both directions). Continue going back and forth until the work is a cylinder; as the roughing proceeds, the cut faces get bigger, the gouge spends less time in thin air and the noise and feel of the cut smooth out. Play with the angles of the gouge to find the best combination. You can check progress while the lathe is running by placing your thumb lightly on the work (in a trailing position, with the thumb pointing in the direction the work is going) and feeling for the remaining flat surfaces.

Sometimes you will need to leave part of the work square (a 'pommel'), as with the top of a table leg. Make a knife cut with the skew chisel to form the transition from square to round before starting the roughing. Having marked the relevant point on the work in pencil (draw a line all the way across at least one side for it to be visible as the work turns), place the skew chisel on the tool rest with the long point down and the handle level. Push the point into the wood; the taper of its bevels limits how far it will go in without an angled relieving cut being made on the side that is to be roughed. Do not push it too hard or the point will overheat.

Continue alternating knife and relieving cuts until those on each corner of the work join up in the middle of each side. Then use the roughing gouge; in order to rough up to the pommel you will need to roll the gouge right over on one side, straighten it up and perhaps raise the handle a little so that you are cutting with one corner of the blade.

Cutting Slots
Either the parting tool or the bedan is used, the latter giving a wider slot of about 10mm. The placing and the depth of slots may be judged by eye or worked out from a drawing and measured. An easy way to cut slots of known depth is to set a pair of calipers to the desired diameter and rest them against the bottom of the slot as it is being cut. When their diameter is reached, the calipers slip over the work and you stop. Repeating the same initial placing and depth of slots is one of the keys to making sets of matching turnings.

Using the tool as a scraper, set the tool rest so that the tip of the tool contacts the work just below the centreline when the tool is angled down 15 degrees or so. Push the tool into the work; the cut will be quite coarse, but quickly made as long as the tool has a good edge. Use a higher speed for this and all subsequent

Cutting a slot with the bedan, with callipers set to slip over as the right depth is reached.

processes; select the speed to suit the average diameter of the work.

Using the Skew Chisel
The basic principle of the skew (and of all chisels and gouges) is that the bevel rubs along the wood that has just been cut and stops the cutting edge from digging in (rather like the sole of a plane), as well as giving the work a slight burnish. The angles at which tools are presented are designed to ensure that the bevel does rub, and, if the tool digs in, it is almost certainly because these angles are wrong.

Starting to cut a taper with the skew.

Continuing the taper. The 'step' by the tailstock centre is a target for the bottom end.

Planing a cylinder with the skew uses a part of the blade between the centre and the short point (unless you are planing into a corner, in which case you must use the short point itself, because it gets there first). It is easiest with the tool rest slightly raised, but, if this is not possible, centre height will do. Angle the tool at about 30 degrees in the direction you are going to go, with the short point leading, so that the cutting edge makes an angle of about 45 degrees to the axis of the work. Rest the tool on the moving work with the back of the bevel running on it and the cutting edge itself just clear; then draw the tool back and raise the handle until the edge meets the work and a wisp of a shaving appears. The bevel should now be lying on the work and, if you set off along the tool rest, the tool should start to plane. A further tiny lift of the handle or roll in the direction you are going will give you a heavier cut. Lift too far and the bevel will lift off the work and the blade dig in, as it will if the long point is allowed to touch the surface of the work.

To cut a convex shape, first cut a slot with the parting tool or bedan (unless the curve is to be on the end of the work). Start to plane a centimetre or two away from the slot and roll the tool, holding it firmly down and raising the handle. The edge of the slot should be rounded over. Repeat the process, starting the roll a little sooner and the curve should become a little bigger.

Cutting the cove with a gouge.

Always cut 'downhill', from a large diameter down to a smaller one. If you have problems with digging in (much less of the bevel is now able to rub on the work), try cutting with the short point – the finish will not be quite as good, but you should not dig in. To turn a ball shape – in a table leg, for example – start by turning the cylinder to the right diameter. Cut two slots about this diameter apart and mark an 'equator' halfway between (this pencil line should remain intact, to be removed by sanding later). Then round over each half of the ball, trying to keep them symmetrical. This takes a lot of practice. The skew chisel is sometimes used for roughing, particularly on slender, springy spindles; the process is the same as planing.

Using Gouges

Cutting deep concave shapes between centres involves a sort of scooping action – rather like getting ice cream out of a tub. As with convex forms, the cut is always taken from a large diameter to a smaller one, so the two sides of the cove are cut separately. To cut the right-hand side, roll the spindle gouge almost 90 degrees to the left; put it on the rest on a point opposite the bottom of the intended cove. Starting to cut just to the right of the middle, scoop down, rolling the gouge as you go, so that when you reach the bottom it is facing straight up. Then roll the gouge 90 degrees to the right and take a cut from the left-hand side in the same way. Keep cutting from alternate sides until the cove is of the desired size.

The use of a bowl gouge on faceplate-mounted work involves different techniques. In contrast to between-centres work, the outsides of bowls are cut 'uphill', from small to large diameter. The angle at which the tool is presented to keep the bevel rubbing is much more dependent on the shape of the work. Although the 'inboard' side of the lathe may theoretically have enough room to swing the size of bowl you wish to turn, the lathe bed will probably interfere with the gouge handle.

The finished leg.

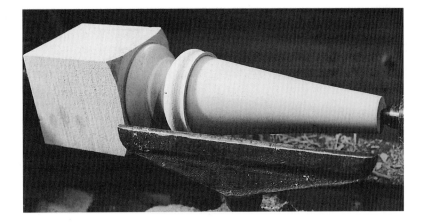

Details

These can be applied with a skew, with smaller chisels or with a form tool. The latter and any other scrapers work best on very hard wood; details in softwood are vulnerable.

When a spindle has been turned very thin and becomes whippy, the action of any tool near the middle of the work sets up vibrations that make normal turning impossible and may even break it. There are two possible solutions. The first is to use a steady – these can be bought or simply made from scrap wood – which supports the work somewhere near the middle and stops it from deflecting away from the pressure of the tool. The second is to wear a clean leather glove (such as a new welding gauntlet) on one hand. Support the back of the work by curling your fingers over the top of it as it turns; the thumb can be used to support the tool.

Finishing

With care and sharp tools, work can be produced with a high polish that needs no further finishing, if this is what you want. But, as noted above, if it is to be painted, a sanded surface provides a better key and takes the paint more consistently. If you are using sandpaper to correct or refine the shape of your turning, start with 80 or even 40 grit. Wear goggles and a dust mask and move the tool rest out of the way. Sanding generates a lot of heat and it may be necessary to wear leather gloves. Otherwise, start with 120 or 180 grit. Apply the paper to the underside of the work, with the palm upwards, or to the top with the paper held so that it trails on the moving work. If you need a finer finish, move on to 240 or 320 grit. Finishes that involve a brush coat followed by rubbing down, such as shellac, should be applied while the work is still in the lathe, if time allows. These finishes are the starting point for giving softwood turnings the appearance of richer materials. Likewise, any filler used to repair damage should be rubbed down on the lathe if possible.

Parting Off

This is necessary when the work has been turned on the end of a larger bit of stock. The parting tool is used either as a scraper or as a chisel and pushed steadily into the work at the required point. Where the surface produced by the parting tool will be a base, as with something such as a candlestick, push the tool in at a very slight angle, rather than dead square, to make the base concave and ensure the best possible stability. Work usually breaks away just before the parting tool severs it in the middle and, when it is delicate, is best supported by a gloved hand as it parts away.

3 WORKING WITH MILD STEEL

Steel on stage: this truck had to carry up to ten performers as well as crates and dressing. The front wheels turn 90 degrees in either direction. The Grapes of Wrath, GSMD; designer: Belinda Akerman; photograph: Laurence Burns.

The ability to weld mild steel makes it possible to build quick, durable, fire-resistant structures. Joints can quickly be made in it that approach the strength of the material around them, and it can be bent to form curves. Although weight for weight it is theoretically

no stronger than wood (along the grain), it can be formed into efficient hollow sections and its greater density means that the same strength comes in smaller packages. It is predictable, having no knots or grain.

The disadvantages are that it is more difficult to alter or to fix other materials to it, costs more and is not suited to elaborate shaping. The object of this chapter is to cover the fundamentals of buying, cutting, and shaping steel, some low-tech ways of bending it, and the MIG welding process as used in small workshops.

CHOOSING AND BUYING STEEL

Steel is supplied in a huge variety of sections, described by their means of manufacture – such as 'cold-rolled', and their shape, for instance, RHS (rectangular hollow section). The price you pay depends on a number of factors and usually you will have to telephone for a quotation. Most suppliers will give you a stock list, which tells you what is available (though unlisted sizes may be obtainable). Keeping a record of the prices you pay for different sections enables you to budget, to design economically and to shop around if need be. Most suppliers have minimum orders and free delivery thresholds; it is worth keeping a stock of the sections you use most and hanging on to odd bits of unusual ones.

Among the more useful sections are ERW tubes for light structural work and small solid sections such as round, square and flat bar for detailed work. ERW stands for electrical resistance welded and refers to lightweight tubes – the kind of material that office furniture is made of – that have been formed by folding sheet material and closing it into tube form with a continuous resistance weld. It is available in rectangular, round, and elliptical hollow sections from a few millimetres to around 50mm wide and in wall thicknesses from 1 to 2mm; often in the United Kingdom it is still sold in imperial sizes with the wall thickness expressed

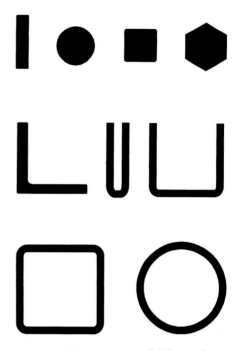

Common steel sections, available in a huge range of sizes. Top row: flat, round, square and hexagonal bars. Middle: angle, narrow U section (sold as edging strip for expanded metal) and channel. Bottom: square and round tubes.

in gauge numbers. It comes in lengths of 6.1 or 7.5m.

Flat bars and wires come in a wide variety of sizes and finishes, mostly in 6.1m lengths. Buy 'black' steel for normal use (the more expensive 'bright' steels are precision engineering materials). Angle sections may also be useful, particularly for making small brackets for joints to timber or other steelwork.

DEGREASING, MARKING AND CUTTING

Steel is supplied coated with grease to prevent rusting. The first thing you need to do is to remove this coating; if you leave it, it will get all over your hands and clothes, and be burnt off in the welding process, producing fumes. While there are proprietary products for this, the cheapest and most benign way is to use the economy washing-up liquid sold by supermarkets. If you have the room, degrease whole lengths before cutting them up; otherwise cut them into manageable pieces first. Lay the steel on trestles somewhere where a little water will not matter – this is a wet process! Cover a rag liberally with washing-up liquid and smear it all over the steel, rubbing it well in to dissolve all the grease. Then, with a clean rag and a bucket of warm water, rinse the steel well, renewing the rag and water as necessary. It is not really necessary to dry the steel: light rust may form in places but can easily be removed with a wire brush if necessary.

For really accurate work, mark up the steel with a scriber or some other hard steel point. This scratches a precise, bright line into the

A small metal-cutting bandsaw in action.

A cold-cut saw being used to chop scaffolding tube.

Using an angle grinder.

surface. On polished surfaces such as ERW the mark may be hard to see: use a marker pen first and scratch into that. Where accuracy is less important, typewriter correction pens and marker pens both work well on all kinds of steel. Setting-out tools – squares, gauges and so on – may be the same as those used for wood, although grime and grease picked up from steel and then transferred to wood may be hard to remove. The basic hand tool for cutting up steel is a hacksaw with a blade of 18 teeth per inch, and every workshop should have one. But any appreciable amount of metalwork will require something faster. Machines that cut with an abrasive disc are the cheapest, and there are two kinds: hand-held angle grinders and bench-mounted cut-off machines. Both cut quickly, but are extremely noisy and leave a ragged edge

that needs a lot of cleaning up. Cold cutters, bench-mounted machines that cut with a circular blade lubricated with cutting fluid, are slower but make a much cleaner cut. Mechanical hacksaws and small horizontal metal-cutting band saws both produce a clean cut, but rather slowly. Once the cut has been started, however, they may be left to get on with it, while you mark up the next piece, put the kettle on or whatever. Larger vertical band saws are expensive industrial machines, although, like their woodworking cousins, they are not well suited to cutting long lengths to size.

Other hand tools include snips and shears for cutting thin sheet, bolt croppers for flat bar and small round and square sections, and the traditional cold chisel and hammer, for tight corners where other tools will not reach.

53

All cutting equipment, to a greater or lesser extent, leaves a burr or ragged edge that can cut you badly and interferes with the fit of parts for welding. It should therefore be removed, soon after cutting, with a file, small grinder or hand-held belt sander.

SHAPING AND DRILLING TOOLS

In a small-scale props workshop the most useful shaping tool is a hand-held angle grinder (so-called because the axis of the disc is at a right-angle to the motor and the body of the tool). This comes in two sizes: those designed to take a disc 110 or 125mm in diameter, and those about twice that size. Both sizes can be used with thin cutting discs, as mentioned above, or with thicker grinding discs, for processes such as grinding welds flat or preparing joints. These tools are hardly precision instruments, and the sparks they produce and the discoloration of the steel due to the heat they generate may make marks hard to follow. The larger versions in particular are powerful tools and can take

Working Safely with Grinders

Never use cutting discs for grinding. Always wear ear defenders and goggles; gloves can protect your hands against sparks. If there is any chance that the work may move, clamp it down or hold it in a vice. Be aware of where the sparks are going; protect others and guard against fire by placing barriers to contain the sparks if necessary. Be aware that the work can become very hot and that very sharp edges may be formed.

ABOVE: Cut ends of steel before and after deburring.

Using a belt sander to remove burrs. The steel is held so that it trails in relation to the movement of the belt.

some getting used to, but their versatility makes them worth the effort.

Tasks such as removing burrs from freshly cut steel can be done more quickly and cleanly with a small, hand-held belt-sander – ideally one that can be used in one hand. Hold small pieces of work in the other hand, ensuring that they are 'trailing' in relation to the belt to avoid kicks; rest them or the sander on the edge of a bench if you need to. Coarse belts – 40 or 60 grit – cut the fastest, while everything finer than 80 grit just polishes your work. Sanders do not remove steel nearly as fast as grinders, but leave a much smoother finish and do not produce the same shower of sparks; they are also quieter.

Files of all shapes and sizes can be useful for cleaning up cut edges and getting into awkward places where the grinder or sander will not go. 'Bastard' files remove metal the fastest, but leave a coarse finish, while 'second cut' and 'smooth' are progressively slower and finer. Apart from needle files, which have integral handles, all files should have wooden or plastic handles fitted to them for safety; never hold them by the tang alone.

Drilling into or through mild steel is done with HSS (high-speed steel) bits in either hand-held electric drills or floor- or bench-mounted pillar drills. Some cordless drill/drivers are powerful enough for smaller diameter bits, although usually only two speeds are on offer. A number of factors affect the success of drilling. First, the bits must be sharp – blunt edges need more pressure to make them cut, leading to overheating of the bit. Secondly, bits cut best at the correct speed, which for HSS in mild steel is when the outside edge of the drill bit is moving through the work at about 30m/min. This gives an ideal drill speed of 3,200rpm for a 3mm bit, and 800rpm for a 12mm bit. Pillar drills intended for metalwork offer a wide range of speeds, and many modern hand-held drills have continuously variable speeds from 0 to around 3,000 rpm; older hand-held drills,

Drilling steel in a pillar drill.

however, may offer only two speeds, making them less suitable for this kind of work. It is running the bits too fast that should be avoided – run too slowly they just take longer – so, if you don't have a wide range of speeds available to you, it is your maximum size of hole that will be limited. Lastly, the bit should be lubricated; a 10 per cent mixture of soluble oil or cutting fluid with water reduces friction and helps the swarf to clear. Apply it frequently from an oil-can or a plastic bottle.

To prevent the drill bit from wandering across the work, use a hammer and a centre punch or a spring-loaded, automatic punch, to 'pop' a

55

conical dent at the mark for the hole. This also helps to start the bit cutting – the chisel edge at its point generates less cutting power on a flat surface. With larger bits, where the pop mark is not big enough to initiate cutting and prevent wander, a pilot hole must be drilled of suitable size. Go from, say, a 5mm pilot hole to a 12mm bit; with a hand-held drill an intermediate hole of 8 or 9mm would help to control the break-through that comes at the end and is the most hazardous part of using such a drill. 'Bullet point' bits, with a small pilot drill at the point of a larger bit, are efficient but awkward to sharpen. Always use the drill two-handed, with a side-handle for the supporting hand. Make sure that the work is held in a vice or otherwise restrained; if the only option is to clamp for work between your boot and the floor, make sure that you wear a steel-toe-capped boot, and that you are well-balanced; the risk of back injury is high.

With a pillar drill, the risk of 'snatching' is less, as long as the work is clamped to the table of the drill or held in a vice clamped to it. Holding small pieces of work down with your hand alone is very dangerous. The whole drill bit should be enclosed by a telescopic, clear plastic guard; wear goggles in any case and be aware of the danger to hands from hot, sharp swarf; clear and dispose of it regularly (but not with your bare hands). Clean up the sharp edges of newly-drilled holes with a light touch with a counter-sinking bit or a larger drill bit. Countersinks for screw heads are neatest when made with a special bit, although a large, old drill bit reground to a 90-degree included angle cuts faster and is easier to sharpen.

BENDING CURVES IN STEEL

One of the great advantages of steel is that it can be bent to form curves. Although it bends much more readily when red hot, a surprising amount of work may be done cold, which is quicker, cheaper and safer. The industrial machine for this work is called a ring roller, and if the steel section you want to bend is too strong, the work large or you need great accuracy, then you should farm out your bending to someone with one of these. Your steel supplier may be able to arrange this. However, you can do more delicate work yourself with a bit of muscle and some plywood formers around which to bend the steel.

As you start to bend a piece of steel, you must pull it to its elastic limit before it starts to deform permanently. When the bend has been made and you let go, the force that took up the elasticity is removed, and the steel springs back a bit. This means that, in order to bend a piece of steel into a semi-circle, you actually have to bend it into slightly more than one, and of a tighter radius than the one you want, to allow for the spring-back. Thus there is much trial-and-error involved in cutting the plywood formers. One approach is to cut the former to the inside shape of the curve that you want, bend a piece of steel

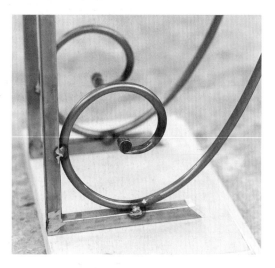

Hand-bent scrolls on a piece of furniture.

RIGHT: *A chandelier with arms bent from ½in ERW tube. Il Giovedi Grasso, GSMD; designer: Charlie Edwards; photograph: Laurence Burns.*

around it, and see how much it springs back. Cut a corresponding amount off your former, erring on the side of caution; bend a fresh piece, and check it against a drawing. Repeat the process until you get the shape you want. With experience, you may find that you can draw roughly the right shape directly.

The Basic Set-up

Whatever the curve you are bending, you will need the following equipment:

* a strong wooden bench or table, preferably fixed to the floor, with a level, clear top;
* a full-size drawing of your desired curve;
* scrap plywood at least as thick as the steel you are bending, to make the former;
* compasses, trammels or a flexible ruler for drawing the former, and a jigsaw or band saw for cutting it out;

* strong screws (number 10 or 12), a drill and a screwdriver (electric or pump);
* pieces of scrap wood;
* goggles and gloves.

You will need some pieces of steel to get the shape right; how many depends on how complex it is. Cut them with plenty of extra length, until you know how little extra you can get away with. Make sure that the cut ends are completely free from burrs or sharp edges.

Bending a Semicircle

Mark out a circle of the right radius on a piece of 18mm plywood and draw a straight line across it passing through the centre point. Cut out the whole circle and screw it (clamps tend to get in the way) securely to the table. Mark out another semicircle elsewhere on the table or on another piece of ply to refer to.

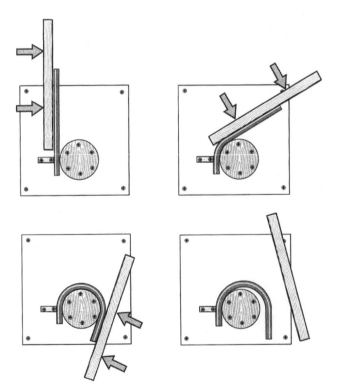

Four steps in bending a semicircle.

Fix a block of wood to trap one end of the steel tight against the circle. Both this block and the former need to withstand a great deal of sideways pressure. Push one end of the first length of steel into the gap. Take a metre of fairly robust timber and place it against the length of steel. Pulling or pushing the wood firmly towards the middle of the circle, roll it around the former; the steel is forced to bend with it. Release the pressure and let the steel spring back.

Take the steel off the jig and compare it with the drawing. Estimate how much smaller the former needs to be; unscrew it, mark a new circle and cut it out. Reattach it to the table, ensuring that the gap that traps the end of the steel remains tight. Then bend a fresh piece and compare this with your drawing. You will probably have to repeat the process several times before you get the curve exactly right. Even though it gets quicker with practice, if all you need is one piece of steel bent to a certain radius it can be a rather long-winded process. In this case, try bending it round a former that you know will be slightly too small; then take hold of the two ends and force them apart, opening up the curve until it fits the drawing. But if you have many identical pieces to make, it will be worth finding the exact size of former required.

Bending an 'S' Curve

The two parts of the curve will each need their own former. Trace the drawing on to the table and on to a piece of plywood. Cut out a former for each part of the curve and fix it to the table.

In this case the steel is trapped, not against a wooden block, but between the two formers. Make sure that there is enough 'overlap' between them to do this. Bend in the same way as before. Sometimes, the steel tends to slip around the former; the best way to stop this is for two people to work opposite each other, bending the two parts of the curve simultaneously.

It is more difficult to adjust these formers for spring-back, particularly if they are not parts of

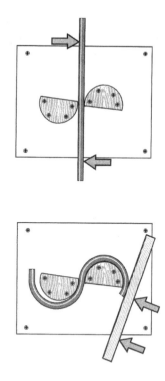

Set-up for bending an S-curve.

circles. One curve must flow seamlessly into the other. Do not cut anything away from the overlap zone; use the same screw holes to fix the formers back down. Tighten the curves with a flexible ruler, re-cut them and try another piece of steel. As with the semicircle, the steel 'blanks' should be cut well over length; after the piece has been successfully bent, its ends can be marked up from the drawing and trimmed.

Hoops

There are two ways to make full circles. The first is to use an undersized former and allow the steel to spring back, as described above. The second is to use a full-size former. In this case, the steel is bent around the former until the two ends overlap; a mark is made across both pieces at the overlap and the ends are cut off. The steel is then placed on the jig; the two ends are forced together and joined with a weld. Gaining access to the weld site may be difficult on a plywood jig; it is important that the weld is strong enough to overcome the spring-back now trapped in the hoop or it will not be truly circular once removed from the former. In both methods the two ends of the steel must overlap each other. The former therefore needs to be at least twice as thick as the material being bent.

Limitations

The size of the solid section you can bend, or the tightness of the curve you can bend it to, depends on how big it is and on how strong you and your workbench are. The situation with hollow sections is more complex: some are just too strong to bend; perversely, others may be too weak.

What is happening when the steel is bent is that the part on the inside of the curve is compressed, while that on the outside is stretched. In thin-walled tubes the compression of the wall nearest to the former may lead to the formation of little ripples; once this happens a weak point is created there, and the tube buckles catastrophically instead of forming a fair curve. In all bending operations these forces cause the sides of the steel to bulge out to some extent. If this matters to you, have your bending done on a ring roller, where such distortion is minimal.

MIG WELDING

Of the handful of welding processes suitable for small-scale manual work, the most common is MIG (metal inert gas). At a basic level, it is the technique most easily learnt, and although manual metal arc equipment is cheaper to buy and to run, MIG is capable of greater delicacy and usually produces fewer fumes and less UV radiation.

'Metal' indicates that the necessary heat is produced by an arc between the work and a piece of metal (which also supplies filler metal for the weld), and 'inert gas' that the molten

Welding in progress. The welder's head is positioned to one side of the arc for a better view and to avoid the rising fumes.

steel is shielded from reacting with atmospheric oxygen by an envelope of gas. In fact, many shielding gas mixtures do react with the welding process in some way, and the term MAG (metal active gas) is also used. The American term GSMA (gas-shielded metal arc) is a better general description.

In MIG welding there are two distinct ways of transferring the filler metal to the work: dip and spray. In spray transfer, high voltage and current maintain a continuous arc; the rate at which filler metal is deposited is high and the weld-pool is very hot and fluid. In dip transfer, although the arc appears continuous, it is actually intermittent. As a result, much less heat is involved; filler transfer is slower and vertical or overhead welding is possible. Smaller transformers may be used to produce the lower voltage/current combinations required. All references to MIG welding in this chapter refer to dip transfer.

How MIG Welding Works

When the trigger on the torch is squeezed, three things happen. A valve opens and the shielding gas starts to flow; filler wire starts to emerge from the torch; and a current from the transformer is fed into the wire via the copper tip through which it passes.

Assuming that the voltage and the wire speed are set correctly and that the torch is the right distance from the work, the following sequence of events then takes place:

1. The wire advances until it touches the work; the electric circuit is completed; the end of the wire heats up and explodes like a fuse wire; the molten part is transferred to the work.
2. An arc appears between the work and the remaining end of the wire, producing heat; the wire continues to advance through this arc until it touches the work; the arc shorts out, the wire again heats up, and the sequence repeats itself.

ABOVE: ***A MIG welding machine.***

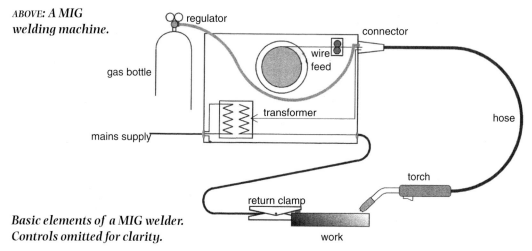

Basic elements of a MIG welder. Controls omitted for clarity.

This happens around a hundred times per second, which is why the arc appears to be continuous. The heat from the arc and from the melting wire is sufficient to melt the two sides of the work and to fuse them together with the filler wire. The intermittence of the arc means that the heat input is small in comparison with other welding processes. While this minimizes distortion and allows delicate work be done, it also leads to the fusion problems associated with MIG welding. To learn to recognize and avoid these and to acquire all but the most basic skills, you should ideally seek training from someone competent, as well as reading

MIG Welding Safety

A number of serious hazards are involved, though all can be minimized by taking the right precautions.

Electrocution
Although the voltages involved are low, the currents are not. You risk electrocution if you offer the welding current a better path either to earth or back to the transformer than is otherwise available to it. Never work in damp conditions. Wear leather gloves and insulating soles. Inspect machine, hose and torch regularly and do not use if any are damaged. Never touch the tip or wire while the machine is switched on. If possible, attach the return clamp to the work itself, not the bench, and make sure there is a good electrical contact.

Damage to the Eyes and Skin
The arc produces intense radiation at infrared, visible and ultraviolet wavelengths that can burn your skin and seriously damage your eyes. Always wear an approved full-face mask with the right filter – BS 679 11/ or 12/EW. Always wear leather welding gauntlets and non-inflammable overalls, and ensure that the skin at the forearms and neck is protected. Always use screens to make sure that no one can see the arc. Place notices to warn others that the work is going on.

Damage to Lungs and Throat from Fumes
The fumes produced by MIG welding are mostly tiny particles of the metal itself, plus the products of burning off any coatings such as grease or old paint. These should therefore be thoroughly removed. Although the metal fumes produced by dip transfer MIG welding of mild steel should be within safety limits, it is nevertheless best to extract fumes at source; if this is not possible, a suitable particle mask should be worn – ask equipment suppliers or manufacturers. Keep your head out of the rising plume of fumes.

Burns
This process produces much heat: the temperature of the arc can be up to 4,000°C. The steel in the area of the weld may remain hot for a long time, and splatters of molten metal may be thrown out from the weld. Always wear leather welding gauntlets and do not leave any skin exposed. Wear a skullcap if necessary to protect the top of the head. Do not allow others into the immediate area unless they are involved in the work.

Fire
Your clothing and your environment are at risk from splatter. Wear non-flammable overalls and a leather apron for heavy work. Use an all-steel workbench. Work in non-inflammable, clean surroundings; keep the area clear of drawings and other clutter. A suitable fire extinguisher and a fire blanket must be at hand. Inspect the area for an hour after you stop welding.

specialist textbooks. The introduction to basic practice that follows is no substitute for either of these.

Equipment

MIG machines are rated by the maximum amperage they can produce. Machines up to 180A are available to run on a single-phase supply, although those over 140A may require a 20A outlet rather than an ordinary 13A socket. A 140A machine taking up to 0.8mm wire is adequate for most prop making purposes; one of 180A would be better for very frequent use. Beware of the small 'no-gas' machines that are popular with hire companies. They use a flux-cored wire instead of a shielding gas; the gases produced by the burning flux mean that they almost certainly require local exhaust ventilation.

Shielding gases are available in small quantities in disposable canisters; to obtain anything bigger you will need an account with an industrial gas supplier. There is a hire charge for the bottle and you pay for the gas itself, as well as an administrative/delivery charge, each time you get a fresh bottle. The standard shielding gas for mild steel is argon, with 5 to 25 per cent carbon dioxide and a small amount of oxygen; the less carbon dioxide the thinner the gauge of steel the gas is intended for. An argon regulator with a flow meter should be fitted. Unscrew the knob on the regulator until it is slack at the end of each session to relieve the diaphragm spring.

A basic welding mask is a plastic face shield fitted with a dark green glass filter; a piece of plain glass protects the filter from splatter, and the whole thing pivots on an adjustable headband. Tipped up out of the way for normal vision, it needs to be lowered into place immediately before welding – with a free hand or a nod of the head. Masks are available with filters that are clear under normal light but darken immediately the arc is struck. These are

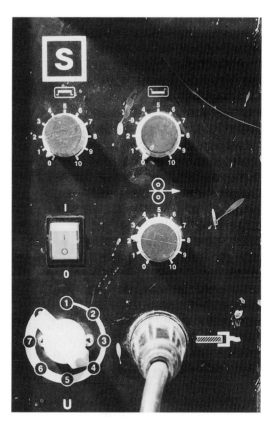

MIG controls. Top: two timing switches for semi-automatic welding. Middle: on-off switch and wire speed control. Bottom: arc-voltage selector.

much more expensive, but make life a lot easier. Other necessary equipment includes insulated side cutters or pliers for trimming the wire and a wire brush for the final cleaning of the parts to be welded.

Voltage and Wire Speed Settings

The size of the weld and the energy of the arc can be varied to suit different thicknesses of steel by adjusting the arc voltage. Once a voltage has been selected, the wire speed is adjusted to produce a stable arc. If the speed is set too

Joint Preparation

Any paint or coating should be removed for at least 100mm from the area to be welded. New steel should not need any surface preparation as long as it is free from rust and grease, but it can be ground or sanded for critical work. To aid penetration when the steel is over 2mm thick, a small gap can be left between the parts to be welded. If the dimensions are critical, make allowances when cutting parts to length. Alternatively, grind an angle of 30 degrees or so on to each part. The rounded edges of rectangular

hollow sections also help the weld to penetrate. Thicknesses over 5mm need both a ground 'V' and a root gap.

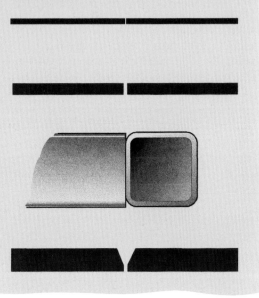

Joint preparation to ensure good penetration. Steel up to 2mm can be butted; over this thickness a small gap is left. The rolled edge of rectangular tubes also aids penetration. Over 5mm thick, a V of 60 degrees included angle and a small 'root gap' are advisable.

low, the wire will burn back to the tip when the first arc is struck; if it is too high, it advances more quickly than it can be melted and the end is felt 'stubbing' against the work.

The voltage is increased in steps, while the wire speed is continuously variable. The numbers used to indicate different settings do not refer to actual mathematical units. The right settings for different thicknesses of steel on a particular machine will be learnt by trial and error. As a rough guide a good voltage for 1.5mm steel will probably be about halfway up the range of available settings on a 120A or 140A machine, and around a third of the way up on a 180A machine. When experimenting with the wire speed, try starting too high and reducing it until the right setting is found.

Getting Ready to Weld

1. Clear the area of inflammable materials; place screens and warning notices if required; make sure a fire extinguisher and fire blanket are at hand.
2. Make sure that you are wearing boots, overalls and an apron, and that gauntlets, a welding mask and a dust mask are at hand.
3. Connect the welder to the power source, but do not switch on at its on-off switch yet.
4. Connect the return clamp to the work as near as is practicable to the part to be welded.
5. Open the valve on the gas bottle (about half a turn on industrial bottles) and screw in the regulator knob until it shows 10–15ltr/min.
6. Switch on the machine and set the voltage and the wire speed if they are not already set.

7. Put on the face mask, dust mask and gauntlets.
8. Trim the wire if necessary with insulated cutters.
9. Drop the mask down over your face and weld.

Making a Horizontal Butt Weld

1. Hold the torch with the shroud vertical or nearly so. The end of the shroud should be about 10mm above the work. If possible, use both hands to support the torch; find a position where you have a good view of the weld.
2. Squeeze the trigger, holding it in, and hold the torch steady as the arc starts. Keep it stationary for a fraction of a second while a puddle of molten metal builds up.

3. Slowly and steadily, maintaining the same distance between the shroud and the work, move along the joint. The arc should always be between the wire and the work, leading the weld pool.
4. When you want to finish the bead, stop moving the torch. Hold it still for another brief moment before releasing the trigger to extinguish the arc.

Common Faults with First Welds

✳ Moving too fast: a thin bead of weld with a round profile lies on the surface of the metal.
✳ Moving too slowly: the bead is large but with poor fusion, as the arc was aimed at the weld pool, not the work itself.

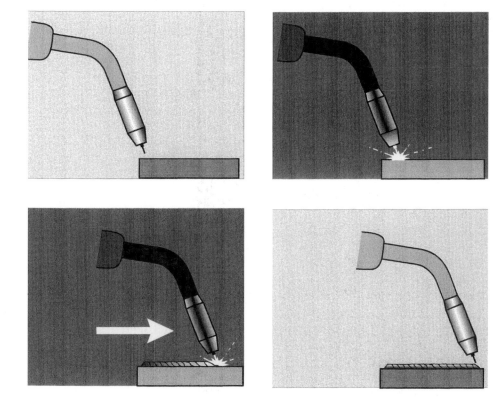

Four steps in laying down a bead of weld.

* Current too high: the weld is very wide with a shallow or flat profile, and the arc may burn through the steel.
* The torch is too close: the arc is small and quiet and may go out, the wire may burn back to the tip, and the end of the shroud may touch the weld and stick.
* The torch is too far away: fusion is poor; the arc is noisy and unstable and splatters a lot.

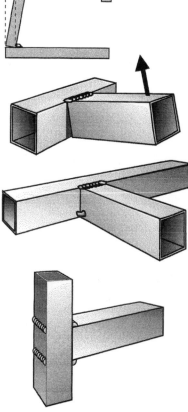

Distortion

Welds shrink as they cool and the resulting distortion needs to be controlled. The simplest way of doing so is by some form of restraint. The parts of the work can be clamped together or to the bench, or simply weighted down. A number of joints in a structure can be tack welded together and its geometry checked, before making full-scale welds over the tacks. It is possible to make, in one fluent action, a couple of tacks on one surface of a joint followed by a full weld along the opposite one. This has the advantages that, if the tacks are then reinforced, a large structure may not need to be turned over, and that the underside has no weld on it to obstruct cladding with plywood or whatever.

LEFT: *The effects of distortion. The angles about a weld tend to close up as the work cools, unless some sort of restraint, such as tack welding, is used. Extra welds (bottom) can correct distortion by balancing the distribution of welds around the tube; they can be ground off later if necessary.*

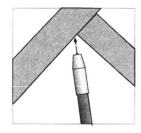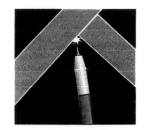

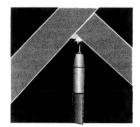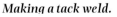

Making a tack weld.

Making Tack Welds

1. Aim the torch at the joint to be welded, and squeeze the trigger.
2. As the arc starts, move it first to one side of the joint and then to the other; release the trigger.
3. The tack should form a small bridge of weld metal, well fused to both sides of the joint.

RIGHT: Close-up of tack and butt welds in 25mm × 25mm × 2mm tube.

BELOW: Making fillet welds.

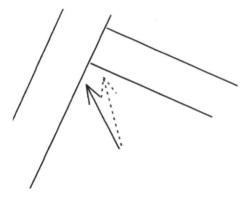

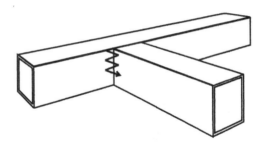

Where one surface is horizontal and the other vertical, tilt the torch over to 45 degrees so that it bisects the angle between the two surfaces; proceed as for butt welds, checking that the weld is fusing equally to both sides.

Where both surfaces are vertical, bisect the angle with the torch pointing horizontally or slightly upwards; small welds can be made either up or down.

Larger vertical fillets should be made by starting at the top of the joint and zigzagging down to stop molten material running down the joint; this motion, called 'weaving', should be regular and rhythmic like a pendulum and may be used whenever you need to control the weld pool against gravity or need a wider weld profile.

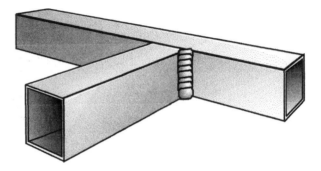

4 MODELLING

This chapter covers modelling with clays, waxes and other materials, and the use of simple armatures for support and reinforcement. It also looks at larger-scale work where the armature becomes closer in shape and size to the finished object, saving weight and material.

Modelled work can either go directly on stage or it can form the original from which a mould is made. In either case, when the modelling is done the material needs to be 'plastic' in the true sense of the word – easily formed into a new shape – and to stay where it is put, with no tendency to bounce back, slowly flow under gravity, or stick to tools. All these properties are difficult to achieve in a modelling compound, and the ease of working of clay, the 'classic' material, is rare.

In other respects materials for direct modelling and for making work for mould-making differ. The former demands something that will cure or dry to a tough, serviceable state, perhaps lightweight or fire retardant. For the latter, the emphasis will be on working properties, an unhurried time scale, and perhaps the possibility of recycling.

Modelling materials are almost never used alone; they are nearly always supported by an underlying structure or surface. The conventional skeletal structure for a free-standing object or figure is called an 'armature', and in

LEFT: *An actor tries on a mask for size and balance.*

large work this may be closely tailored to the shape of the object. The design and construction of such an armature is as important to the success of the work as the modelling itself. But the supporting structure can also be much simpler, like the plywood board on which a clay mask is modelled before moulding, or the half-dozen nails knocked part way into a chair back to give a purchase to a piece of modelled detail.

Like carving, modelling is often seen as a mysterious process, the preserve of people with an innate gift for sculpture. But while it is true that natural talent helps, there are two more essential factors. The first is frequent practice; as with music, a modest natural gift can be developed through hard work, while the greatest talent is useless if you do not apply it. The second is the need to have a clear picture in your head – and preferably also on paper in front of you – of what it is you are trying to make. Work from references whenever possible, and leave sculptural improvisation to those without deadlines to meet or designers to please.

TEMPORARY MODELLING MATERIALS

These are used only for making originals for moulding and casting, and include the most easily modelled and the cheapest materials.

Natural Clay
The low cost, excellent working properties and reusability of natural clay mean that it remains very important. However, unless it is fired to

Clay work ready for moulding.

produce a ceramic object (something outside the scope of this book and of most props workshops), clay never appears on stage; allowed to dry out, it shrinks, cracks and disintegrates. Instead, it should be thought of as a vital intermediary, for making originals to be cast in more suitable materials.

Clay is unsuitable for making very small objects, because they dry out quickly, or for creating fine detail, which needs more resistance; both are easier with oil clays. It comes into its own at a scale where you can work it with your hands, when it models more easily than other materials. For work on a large scale there is no good alternative, unless you can afford large quantities of oil clay or wax. Large work is physically demanding and assumes the technology to build heavyweight armatures in steel and timber.

Working with Clay

Clay, usually grey or terracotta in colour, is available from sculptors' or potters' suppliers in 25kg bags. It is usually supplied sterile and air-sealed, and will last for weeks or even months as long as you do not open or accidentally pierce the bag. Once the bag is opened, the shelf life reduces, and the clay will need regular damp-

ening to keep it useful, and a disinfectant to discourage mould (*see* Recycling Clay below).

The easiest way to cut clay up is with a length of nylon monofilament (fishing line) stretched between the hands. Model, carve and shape it with your fingers or whatever works for you – knives, proprietary wire or wooden modelling tools, or home-made or found tools.

The modelling process may be lubricated by using water, talc or grease. Water tends to soften

OPPOSITE PAGE:
Beginning to model a mask in clay.

TOP LEFT: A rough drawing is made on the surface enabling the basic shapes to be established.

TOP RIGHT: The basic shapes are refined and corrected.

BOTTOM LEFT: Detail is added and the surface worked to the desired texture. Here a spoon is used to form the eyeballs.

BOTTOM RIGHT: The mask ready to be moulded. See pages 87–9.

detail, stick to the hands and make further work more and more muddy. Grease and talc both stop the clay from sticking to your fingers and allow smooth, polished surfaces to be created. The effect of talc is temporary, since the thin lubricating layer absorbs moisture and becomes part of the clay surface; it can be overcome by dampening. This and the fact that it is dry make talc the most useful of the three.

Some work can be done flat on a board, such as the modelling of masks or other flat-backed work; but more free-standing or three-dimensional things will probably need an armature or framework to stop the clay from sagging. For relatively small objects – a life-sized head, for instance – this might be as simple as a wooden upright with a small crosspiece attached, fixed to an 18mm-ply base. Anything larger or more elongated in form will require an armature both stronger in construction and more carefully tailored to the shape of the intended work (*see* Armatures below). Wooden armatures must be painted or varnished if the clay is to stick to them, as must plaster when building up masks on life-cast faces.

During the work it may sometimes be necessary to leave a layer of clay to dry out a little to enable it to harden up, either to prevent sagging when more is added or to minimize damage during mould-making. Most often, though, you will need to protect your clay from drying out; very small pieces of work – and waste – are particularly susceptible. When leaving work over breaks or overnight cover it with a piece of damp muslin and a layer of polythene. As you work, clear waste clay regularly, putting it back in the bag. Disinfectant on the muslin or sprayed on to the work helps to keep unwelcome life-forms at bay.

Recycling Clay

Although it takes up time and space, recycling clay saves waste and is said to improve its working qualities. There are two basic steps: replacing water lost through drying, and working the

Starting to model a helmet. A rough clay mass is built up on a hardboard former that establishes the geometry of the brim.

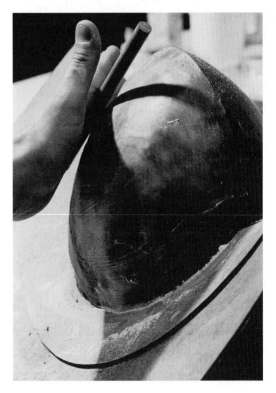

A dowel rod is rolled gently over the surfaces to fair up the curves.

The basic shape finished; clay is rolled out and cut to apply detail.

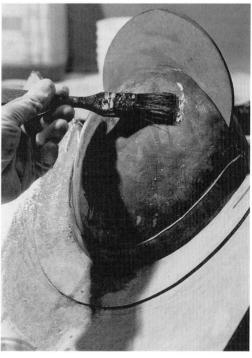

Painting with shellac seals the clay and allows finer surfaces to be created. Talc has a similar effect.

A scrap of lace is pressed into the surface with the rod to suggest engraving.

clay to mix it to an even consistency. The process becomes more difficult the more the clay has been allowed to dry out.

Reclaiming small quantities is straightforward. When the mould is made and the original is finished with, break or cut the clay into small pieces, picking away plaster and other debris, and place these in a bucket along with any waste clay you have saved. Add a small amount of water, perhaps a cupful for every 5kg of clay if it is not too dried out, with a little disinfectant in it. Leave overnight. Then knead the clay with your hands and by repeatedly lifting it and slamming it down on the workbench.

To reclaim larger quantities or clay that has dried out more needs a slightly different

73

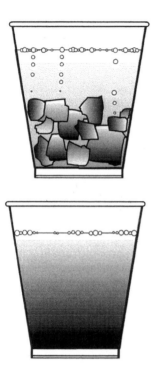

Reclaiming clay.

approach. Break it into pieces and place in buckets or a bin, no more than three-quarters full. This time add enough water to immerse the clay completely, and fill the container right up. Leave to soak for a few days, then siphon off or bale out the clear water on top and mix the clay to a thick slurry with a small spade. The extra water makes the mixing easier, but now needs to be removed to return the clay to a workable state. Spread the slurry out on plywood trays for a few days, turning it over daily, until it has firmed up. If possible, put it through a pugmill; it is hard to achieve the smoothness of new material without one. Otherwise, work it over with the spade or the hands to homogenize it. This is hard work. Store it in heavy polythene bags, tightly sealed, with as much air excluded as possible.

Oil Clays

Oil clays are made by combining dry clay with a mixture of oil and molten wax, and have working properties similar to those of natural clay without its tendency to dry out. There are many products on the market, ranging from the familiar soft and malleable Plasticine to industrial styling clays that are plastic at 50 or 60°C but hard enough to be drilled or machined at room temperature. Some of the latter might be strong enough to use direct on stage, but oil clay is normally regarded as a step towards making a mould. Economical oil clay is easily made in the workshop if you need a large amount; a recipe is given below.

Though its plasticity is not as good as that of natural clay, working with oil clay is a cleaner, more controlled process. The same range of tools can be used, and there is the added factor of temperature – the warmer the clay, the softer it is. Before starting work, prepare your clay by leaving it over a radiator, in a drying cupboard or even in a low oven for long enough for it to soften completely through. The warm clay sticks well to armatures and the initial rough modelling is easier. As the work progresses, it may be necessary to reheat the clay to keep it workable. Long, gentle heating with a hair drier or fan heater softens deep into the clay, while short, fierce heat – as from a hot-air paint stripper – softens just a thin layer at the surface. Alternatively, it is often useful to leave partly-made work to cool and firm up before detail is applied; work may even be put in the freezer to allow it to be carved or machined.

As with natural clay, some kind of lubrication is often useful during modelling. Once again, talc is effective, as are oil, petroleum jelly and soap. All these make new material less likely to stick and should be used in moderation. Liquid lighter fuel (petroleum distillate, petrol) may be used as a solvent, as a bonding agent and for cleaning tools.

Although oil clays are compatible with most mould-making materials and release very

Making Oil Clay

If you need a large quantity of oil clay it is economical to make your own. The following recipe can be adapted as required:

- 2kg microcrystalline wax
- 700g petroleum jelly (Vaseline)
- 800g white mineral oil, such as baby oil (about 1ltr)
- 5kg dry, powdered clay, such as ball clay or white china clay.

Place the wax, petroleum jelly and oil in a bucket and heat gently until all have melted together. The safest way to do this is by placing the bucket in a larger container of boiling water – wax is flammable when molten and should not be melted over direct heat. When the wax has all melted into the oil, stir in the clay, mixing thoroughly. Turn out into plastic containers or damp plaster moulds.

Paraffin wax cannot be used for this recipe since its crystals are large and brittle and the clay produced is crumbly. Using a mixture of microcrystalline wax and beeswax makes a more flexible clay, less prone to cracking when bent, but increases the cost. A mixture of ball or china clay with one of very high plasticity, such as bentonite, makes a softer, finer product, increasing the cost slightly.

cleanly from them, those that contain sulphur should not be used with some urethane and silicone rubbers. Most suppliers can advise on the compatibility of different products.

Modelling Waxes

Like oil clays, waxes take great detail without drying out; some are soft for modelling, others hard enough to be carved, machined or turned. Most mould-making materials part from them without a release agent. Although some contain clay, they rely on the plasticity of the wax/grease mixture; they become totally liquid when heated past a certain point. Most can be cast into moulds to create basic shapes or details to apply to larger work; they can also be melted out of plaster waste moulds before being cast.

Wax can be prepared for use by melting it, then allowing it to cool until it just sets. It is then at its most malleable (molten wax is flammable – see 'Making Oil Clay'). For a supply of small quantities of warm wax, keep a pan of molten material on a very low heat; pour puddles on to a cool surface, scrape up with a blade or filling knife as they set and use immediately. Alternatively, molten wax can be built up in layers by painting on to a core or armature; the heaviest build-up is possible when the wax is just about to set. Detail is often modelled by heating the tools themselves in a flame, which allows for local melting of the wax. Playing a flame over the surface of the wax itself blends details and removes tool marks, creating a uniform, smooth texture.

Waxes, particularly in their pure form, are more difficult to work with than are clay or oil clay, and are best used only when their specific properties are exploited, as in lost-wax casting.

PERMANENT MODELLING MATERIALS

This group of materials may be modelled, but then dry, set or cure to a state that is tough enough to use on stage. This allows direct modelling of objects or of details on larger work. They are not as strong as some casting materials, but often this doesn't matter as long as the prop can survive reasonable wear and tear. Their disadvantages over clay and wax may be high cost or a greater threat to health, both of which also apply to many moulding and casting materials, or just poorer working properties.

These materials may also be used to make originals for moulding or cast into moulds.

Polymer 'Clays'

This family of products includes some of the strongest and most easily worked of permanent modelling materials, and some of the most expensive. They are not really clays at all, but are based on mixtures of vinyl polymers and plasticizers. They remain plastic (though with a short shelf life) until hardened by baking briefly in an oven. It is a great advantage not having an unstoppable setting process and being able to choose when to harden the work, but it does mean that you are limited by the size of your oven.

These are not industrial products, but are aimed at the craft and leisure markets, where they are used for making things such as dolls and jewellery; there are many books and websites dedicated to their use. In props work they are best used for similar small-scale work. Trade names include Fimo, Sculpey and Cernit.

Air-Drying Clays

These are natural clays with some kind of fibrous reinforcement added (often nylon) to reduce cracking as the material dries out. Kneading in a dry additive at the start of work, painting on a liquid at the end or baking can further harden some products. But objects made from air-drying clay remain delicate and the fibre content makes the clay a little less plastic. It is most useful when economy is the overriding consideration.

Epoxy Putty

Two-part epoxy putty compounds such as Milliput are extremely useful both for repairs and for making small objects. They are available from craft and model shops and from plumbers' and builders' merchants. Sticks of epoxy resin and a slow hardener, each also containing fillers and perhaps pigments, are mixed in equal quantity. The mixture becomes extremely hard and strong in a few hours. Freshly mixed material is soft and sticky from the warmth of your (gloved) hands and may be made even softer by warming it on a radiator or with a hair drier – this also speeds the setting. It may be made firmer by cooling in a refrigerator, which extends the working time considerably and improves the modelling properties. Alternatively, freshly mixed putty can simply be left to part-harden, provided that the work can be done quickly enough after that. Water can be used as a lubricant without affecting setting or adhesion to other materials.

Plaster-Based Mixtures

Plaster on its own is difficult to model, but two simple modifications produce a material that is reasonably strong, works easily and is economi-

---

Getting the Best Out of Polymer Clays

- Condition clay thoroughly before use by warming and kneading it.
- Build work up in layers of fairly consistent thickness; if necessary, make an armature or core of screwed up foil to provide bulk.
- If you need to build up bulk with polymer clay, do so in stages, baking each stage.
- Observe the manufacturer's recommended baking schedule – usually 15 to 30min per 6mm of thickness at 130°C.
- *Do not eat or drink while handling polymer clay:* the phthalate plasticizers used in some products are dangerous; do not allow polymer clay props to be used for food or drink and do not use it for things like clay pipes or cigarette holders.
- *Do not bake polymer clay at temperatures higher than 130°C;* use a reliable oven thermometer to check the temperature in several parts of your oven.

An original for a breakaway clock, made with plastic mouldings and modelled plaster over a wooden base. From this a silicone rubber mould was taken and hollow plaster castings made, which were then painted, glazed and fitted with a real clock movement.

cal on a large scale. First, the setting process must be slowed down to give adequate working time; this can be achieved with proprietary retardants such as tri-sodium citrate or simply with vinegar or lemon juice. Secondly, the plaster must be thickened to a consistency suitable for modelling, and here the range of options is much broader:

* Plasters made purely from 'alpha' gypsum need a smaller excess of water to set properly and may be made up to a thicker consistency than 'beta' gypsums or mixtures of the two. Thicker plaster has less tendency to sag;
* Colloidal silica (fumed silica, amorphous silicon dioxide) is widely used in the GRP

industry for thickening resins, and also thickens plaster very efficiently.

* Paper pulp both thickens and strengthens plaster, although it makes fine detail difficult to model; dampen it slightly before mixing in or it will absorb water needed by the plaster.
* Sawdust, polystyrene dust or a mixture of the two (as you might find in a band saw extractor bag) are all cheap and effective for making textures or other rough work; like paper pulp, sawdust should ideally be damp.

The thixotropizing agents sold with polymer plaster systems will not thicken plaster enough for modelling, are hazardous to use with bare hands and increase the cost. Colloidal silica too may be expensive if bought in small quantities – as usual the bulk buyer has an advantage – but an addition of as little as 3 per cent of the weight of dry plaster is effective. It also has other applications around the workshop. It is best to experiment to find a mixture that suits the kind of modelling you want to do, but a typical recipe might be like this:

* 1kg 'alpha' plaster;
* 350g water;
* 0–30g tri-sodium citrate solution (10:1 water to agent);
* 50g colloidal silica.

This has a working time of between 10min and 2hr, depending on the amount of retardant used. The amount of colloidal silica could be decreased by half and a little paper pulp or sawdust added.

Any of these recipes can also be used as a covering for polystyrene.

Paper Pulp

A cheap and (when dry) lightweight and very strong modelling material can be made from paper pulp mixed with paste or glue. It is a traditional, basic material of prop making and many recipes for it exist, using different papers, glues and other additives such as whiting, sawdust and linseed oil.

All share two serious disadvantages. One is the extremely long drying time; for large-scale work it can be measured in weeks. Sunshine and a warm breeze or energy-consuming fan heaters will speed drying somewhat. An essential measure is to make the modelled layer of paper pulp as thin as possible, which means building an open armature or core as close as you can to the shape of the object and covering this with paper and glue before modelling just a detailed surface. A further complication of the long drying time can be the growth of mould: adding a biocide, or using paste that already contains one, discourages this.

The other problem is the tendency of paper pulp to flocculate or gather into small clumps or balls. As well as making both details and smooth surfaces difficult to achieve, paper pulp in this state has less strength. Thorough mixing with a starch binder such as wallpaper paste and a filler powder minimizes these effects.

The shrinkage that accompanies drying is less of a problem as long as the water content is kept to a minimum. If the work is modelled over a rigid core or armature, small cracks or tears may appear as the material dries, but these may easily be filled.

If you use a lot of pulp it is probably worthwhile to buy it; dry pulp is sold in sacks for making paperclay and for building-insulation (the latter comes with a fire-retardant additive). All you need to do with this is mix it with paste and any other ingredients you want. For one-off jobs, however, you can make it yourself: *see* the box opposite.

Other Modelling Materials

A few other materials are occasionally useful in modelling because of their particular properties.

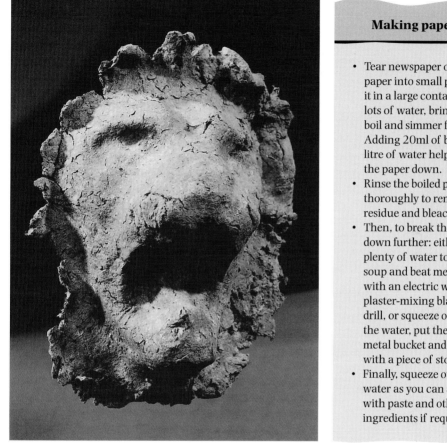

A mask modelled in paper pulp, showing typical texture and drying cracks. In spite of the cracks, this can be a strong material; the main drawback is the extremely long drying time.

Fire Cement

This is sold both industrially and in DIY outlets. Used for building and repairing hearths and furnaces, it is hardened by baking and is then fire-resistant up to around 1,250°C. An object made from it can therefore contain a real fire or survive being placed in one.

The working consistency is a stiff paste, and, with care, detail can be modelled. Light gloves or a barrier cream for wet work should be used to stop it drying your skin out. It is best to work on to a core of expanded metal or scrumpled foil, building up thin layers and baking them hard to support further work when necessary. Bake gently at first – say 30min per centimetre thickness at about 100°C – and then more fiercely, another 30 to 60min at 250°, or hotter if you have a kiln. For decoration, thin some cement with water and use it as a binder for dry pigments; some colours change when heated, so test them if necessary. Metal powders (the kind used for cold casting in resin, not those used to make

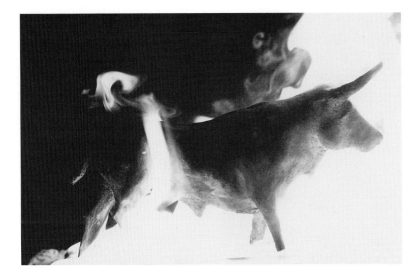

A bull modelled in fire cement over a shell of scrumpled aluminium foil, unaffected by a real fire.

paint) may be mixed with a water/cement paste and 'fired' on, then polished up with wire wool for an effective metallic finish.

Polyester Filler

This is sold for repairing dents in bodywork and as a wood filler, and is a heavily filled polyester resin that comes with a tube of catalyst. It is a difficult material to model but has the advantages of setting rapidly and being easy to carve and sand soon after, making it useful for quick repairs. Use slightly less than the recommended amount of catalyst unless you can work very quickly. You can make a similar material

Modelling thermoplastic splinting material direct over clay.

80

with a general purpose laminating resin catalysed with 0.5 to 1 per cent MEKP and mixed with talc, whiting, dry clay or any other cheap filler (*see* the section on polyester resin in Chapter 6).

Polycaprolactone
This is a low-temperature, thermoplastic polymer that becomes soft enough to model when it is dropped into water at just below the boiling point. It remains workable for a few minutes, hardening as it cools, and can be softened again at any time by reheating. It is not an easy material to model in, with a 'springiness' that precludes fine detail, but is useful for the speed with which basic shapes can be formed and altered, and for its toughness (for more information *see* the section on thermoplastics in Chapter 6).

ARMATURES

Almost all modelled work needs some kind of solid structure inside or behind it to support the modelling material while you work with it. For something that has a flat back, such as a mask or a 'carving' on a piece of furniture, this can be as simple as piling clay on a plywood baseboard or modelling on to the furniture itself. For more fully three-dimensional work, some kind of internal structure will be needed, more or less tailored to the finished shape. This may be an open, skeletal frame (the traditional armature of the clay modeller), a more elaborate structure with a skin of (say) chicken wire, or a core roughly carved or modelled in a lighter material. The open type of armature is more appropriate when making an original for a mould, it is quick to make and the greater quantity of clay needed to fill it out doesn't matter. Skinned armatures and cores take longer to make but reduce the weight, which is important when modelling direct for the stage.

Small-Scale Armatures: Wood, Wire and Foil

A simple open armature for a life-size head is a baseboard of 18mm plywood with a 50mm × 75mm wooden upright fixed in the middle by a couple of stout screws up into the endgrain of the wood. Two short wooden crosspieces are screwed on at right angles to each other to take the clay. Both natural clay and oil clay stick better to wood if it is painted or varnished.

An alternative to the wooden crosspieces which holds the clay better and allows for further refinement is soft aluminium armature wire. This comes in a range of diameters, and although it is thick enough to support the clay without slicing through it, it can be bent into shape with the hands. It is bound together with wire, the square cross-section providing a good grip between parts; larger sizes can be drilled for screwing to timber. Screw-tightening hose clips ('jubilee clips') can also be used to join it to timber or steel. For the life-sized head, two loops of wire are fixed to the wooden upright and the space between them is packed with clay. Further clay is then built on to the outside.

For direct modelling in one of the hardening materials, skinned or core-type armatures save weight and modelling material. Open-frame armatures may be used for small work, but even something the size of a human head is likely to need a core if it is not to be very heavy. Scrumpled kitchen foil, bound or skewered together with wire, is fireproof and absorbs some shrinkage. Scrumpling paper into balls and taping them to a wood or wire structure works well for laminated paper and pulp; roughly carved polystyrene suits all materials apart from polyester putty and those that require oven-baking.

Armatures for Larger Work

Larger open armatures are built from timber, aluminium and flat or tubular steel on the same principles as smaller ones. The strength required of an armature increases with the volume of the work: double the linear dimensions and you need eight times the volume of clay. The weight of a mould may also have to be borne by the armature. Welded steel offers fast, efficient joints and the possibility of bending complex shapes: 20 or 25mm round ERW tube, which can be bent in a manual pipe bender, is a good starting point. Using large-section timber parts or lashing on

Packing clay on to an armature. The chain, stapled to the wooden armature, adds key.

BELOW: *Moose head being modelled on the armature shown above.*

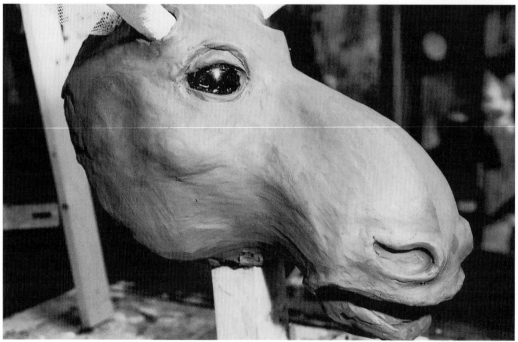

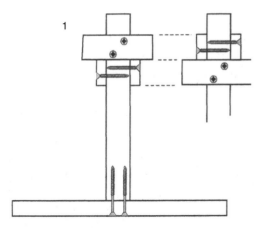

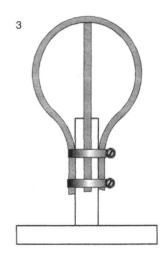

Various head armatures.
(1) Using a ply base, 2in × 2in and 2in × 1in timber.
(2) A variation for elongated heads such as animals.
Wood needs to be sealed with shellac or varnish for
clay to stick.
(3) Square-section aluminium armature wire fixed
to a wooden base with hose clips.

blocks of polystyrene reduces the bulk of the clay. Extra supports from the baseboard add stability; the traditional armature for a standing figure uses a strong third support in an inverted 'L' shape from the base to the small of the back.

Polystyrene continues to be useful for core armatures at larger scales. The main alternative is to make a structure with a skin of chicken wire (for paper-based materials) or expanded metal (for heavier materials).

Chicken wire comes in a range of mesh sizes – 25mm or 1in is the most useful – and can be cut with cheap, serrated scissors. Join it to itself with wire or by entwining the cut ends (which are very sharp) and fix to wooden structures with staples. Getting the first layer of paper to stick may be tricky; try applying glue to the wire, not the paper; once stuck it can be painted with more glue. Scrumpling and unfolding newspaper several times increases its ability to conform to three-dimensional shapes and helps to disguise the pattern of the mesh. Because it is so easy to bend, forms made of chicken wire are not very strong unless the supports are closely spaced.

Expanded metal is available in steel or aluminium in a great range of weights and meshes, and allows much stronger skins to be made. There is a trade-off between strength and the ease with which shapes can be formed by hand, and a good compromise is the lightweight galvanized steel material sold as 'metal lath' by builders' merchants. Cut it with shears or a small grinder and fix to framing with staples or by tack welding (use suitable extraction or protection since zinc is vaporized in the welding process). Join it to itself with twists of wire or with hog rings, soft metal bands applied with special pliers. A first layer of unthickened, unretarded plaster stiffens up the lath so subsequent layers may be modelled on to it.

5   MAKING MOULDS

The use of moulds is of great importance in prop making, for a number of reasons. The most basic is that an original may be created in one material that can easily be modelled, and a cast produced in another material more suitable for use on stage. But moulds also allow existing objects to be copied, difficult or very specific shapes to be created, and, of course, multiple casts to be made.

A lot of the terminology of mould-making is used loosely and can mean many different things. Throughout this book the word mould is used to mean an object providing a 'negative' of the shape of an original object. A material is put against the mould surface that dries or cures to produce a cast of that shape. The whole process is referred to as casting. The expression 'life casting' is used to describe the process of making a mould of a part of someone's body.

TYPES OF MOULD

There are many mould-making materials and many types of mould that can be made from them. Materials range from plaster to synthetic rubber, and techniques from making an impression in a lump of clay to multi-piece rubber moulds supported by rigid cradles. Making

LEFT: *Performer astride a sculptural fragment cast in jute-reinforced plaster in a mould taken from life.* La Calisto, GSMD; *designer: Jamie Vartan; photograph: Laurence Burns.*

complex moulds can be both expensive and time-consuming, and it makes sense to keep things as simple as you can – the time and the money invested in a mould should be in proportion to its usefulness. Planning a mould is best done by envisaging the desired end result and working back from that, considering these a number of key factors.

The shape and texture of the original. First, it is much simpler to make a mould from an original with a base or a back that will not be seen than from one where the whole surface must be reproduced. The mould for the former may well be in fewer pieces and will be easier to fill. Secondly, are there undercuts in the original?

Whether more than one cast is required. If only one cast is needed, could a waste mould – one that is destroyed in the process of removing the cast – be used? This is usually a plaster shell, strong enough to withstand normal handling but still susceptible to being broken away from the cast. Alginate and/or plaster-bandage life moulds also fall into this group (*see* the section on life casting below), as do impressions in clay or wax. Plaster waste moulds get round the problem of undercuts, although the original must be of a soft material such as clay or wax to allow its removal from the mould. The mould may still need to be made in more than one piece to enable the original to be removed and replaced with the casting material. Despite this, waste moulds are cheap and can be quick to make.

Undercuts

These are parts of the shape of an object that can potentially lock it into a mould, and dealing with them is integral to the whole business of casting. They occur in a number of forms:

- When some feature of the shape is simply larger than a part of the mould through which it would have to pass in order to separate the two.
- If two unrelated planes in different parts of the object combine to form an undercut; this type can easily be overlooked.
- As a rough texture – in effect, many tiny undercuts – that can be sufficient to lock a cast into a mould.

There are three main ways to get round the problem of undercuts:

- Use a waste mould, such as a plaster shell, that can be broken away to release the cast.
- Make a piece mould: the mould is divided up so that each individual piece contains no undercuts; this enables a cheap material such as plaster to be used, but requires much skill and patience.
- Use a flexible mould material – this is the solution most often adopted in professional prop making and there are many specialist products on the market.

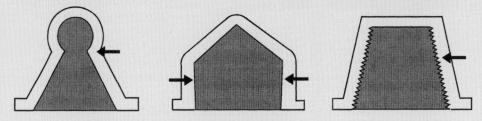

Undercuts: (from left to right) gross undercutting; convergent or parallel surfaces; texture.

The material from which the original is made. Techniques that suit soft clay originals do not necessarily work with rigid materials. Even when made in many pieces, a plaster mould is difficult to release from something like a piece of china; a flexible mould would be a better choice.

The material from which the cast is to be made. If multiple casts are required in rigid materials such as GRP or polymer plaster, the options are either a well-made rigid mould, with a suitable release agent and any undercuts 'designed out' by dividing the mould, or a flexible mould.

Rigid moulds are best used only for small numbers of casts or very simple shapes. Even then easy release relies on some 'spring' in either the cast or the mould: a thin, relatively springy GRP cast can be sprung away from a rigid mould from which a thicker, stiffer cast in the same material would never separate.

The processes involved in making the cast will also influence the design of the mould. Making a hollow cast in GRP, for example, requires easy access to the inside of the mould, while a solid cast needs only a small hole for pouring, and perhaps another to let air escape.

In moulds like this a very runny casting material will flow through smaller openings and into finer detail than a thicker one.

PLASTER

Plaster is a traditional mould-making material, and with earth clay forms the classic combination of soft original and rigid mould. Low price, availability, versatility and safety ensure the continued importance of these materials. Heavy and fragile, they seldom appear on stage, but are vital intermediaries in many casting processes.

The most suitable plaster for mould-making is plaster of Paris, or casting plaster, available from sculptors' or potters' suppliers or from some builders' merchants. Smaller quantities can be bought in chemists or hardware shops. The various types of wall plaster, although widely available, are too slow in setting to be useful for mould-making, except as a last resort. Plasterer's scrim (jute scrim) is used as a reinforcement in thin-walled plaster moulds. It is available in most builders' merchants in rolls 3½in (9cm) wide, and in 36 and 72in (90 and 180cm) widths from sculptors' suppliers.

Other rigid mould-making materials that might be used in place of plaster are GRP (*see* Chapter 6) or plaster/polymer composites such as Jesmonite, either of which will produce stronger, lighter moulds.

Mixing Plaster

Use flexible plastic bowls or buckets to ease the removal of hardened waste plaster. Always test out new plaster for setting time and mix small quantities before mixing large amounts. A mix of 1 part water to 2 or 2½ of plaster by volume is normal. Always place the water in the mixing vessel first; sprinkle the plaster into it, allowing it to settle into the water. Mix with your hand, a mixing stick, or a mixing blade in a drill. The longer and more vigorously the plaster is mixed, the stronger it sets. Setting speed can be accelerated by using hot water or by dissolving salt in the water – up to 10g per litre – or both. A dash of trisodium citrate solution or of glue size will retard it. Only a few millilitres of the former are needed to double the setting time of a litre of plaster, so measure carefully or risk long delays. Do not mix a batch of plaster unless you are ready to use it – it will not wait for you; if a mix starts to go off while you are working with it, abandon it and make a fresh lot. Never put excess plaster down the sink, leave it to set in the bowl and break it out into the bin. Wash your hands and tools in a bucket in the sink and scrape the settled-out sludge into the bin.

Making a One-Piece Plaster Mould from a Clay Mask

1. Make sure that there is a margin of at least 50mm of ply baseboard around the clay work. Paint exposed ply with a thin clay/water mix to stop the plaster from sticking to it. Whether or not you use a release agent on the clay work is up to you: plaster releases more cleanly from clay that has been soaped or sprayed with an aerosol wax, but it is not essential. Soaping destroys fine detail in clay work so that is a situation in which to use a spray.

Equipment for Plaster Moulds

- plaster
- plasterer's scrim
- clean water
- release agent to suit original
- flexible bowls and buckets
- jug or measure
- mixing blade on drill for large work
- scissors
- scraper or knife

Flicking on the first layer of plaster.

Spreading the second layer on when the first has gone off.

2. Mix a small batch of plaster the thickness of double cream and apply a thin layer to the clay work by flicking, pouring or brushing it on. This layer takes up the detail without trapping air bubbles and encases the clay in a layer of pure plaster so that the scrim reinforcement in the next layer does not show on the inside surface of the mould. Scrape excess plaster off the baseboard, leaving a margin of around 30mm around the work. Cut sufficient scrim reinforcement to cover the work completely with an overlap of about 50mm all round, then continue without delay.

3. Make up a larger, thicker mix, and spread it on to the work. Place pieces of scrim one at a time into the wet plaster and work them in with your fingers until they are completely immersed in the plaster. Ensure that each piece is completely wetted out – with the exception of the overlap outside the edge of the work – before going on to the next piece. Continue like this until either you have covered the whole thing, or the plaster starts to go off.

4. At this point start to turn the overlaps back into the wet plaster, using more plaster if necessary to bed them into. Always make sure that scrim is being put into wet plaster; mix up fresh plaster as necessary. (A traditional method is to dip bits of scrim in a bowl of plaster before applying them to the work. In fact, the method described above is far faster and easier, as long as there is always wet plaster for the scrim to go into.) As each

ABOVE: *Working scrim into the wet second layer.*

ABOVE RIGHT: *Turning the overlaps back into the plaster to create a strong edge.*

RIGHT: *The finished mould.*

mix of plaster goes off, scrape any excess from the board – it will come off far more easily now than later.

5. One layer of reinforcement is usually enough for a mask-sized mould, but larger pieces or flattish moulds that do not derive much strength from their shape may need a second layer. Lastly, smooth a small quantity of plaster mix all over the mould to produce a neat, even finish. Wait for the plaster to heat up and cool down again before disturbing it; then turn the whole thing over and pull it away from the baseboard.

6. Hollow out the clay with a clay tool or loop of wire, stopping one or two centimetres short of the mould surface. The remaining clay should peel out in large pieces; if necessary, wash the last bits out. If you need a dry mould, it will take at least 48 hours at room temperature. Moulds can be dried more quickly in an oven or drying cupboard, but may crack if heated unevenly.

Plaster Moulds in More than One Piece

There are two basic ways to do this: the first makes tight-fitting, well registered moulds from any original, while the second is much faster, a rough-and-ready technique for making waste moulds from clay originals.

The clay wall method:

1. Decide where the mould will divide. Build a wall of clay or wax on the dividing line around the piece to be made first. Press something round (like a marble or the end of a screwdriver) into the wall to make registration marks.
2. Make the first part of the mould, using a layer of neat plaster and a layer or two reinforced with scrim, as described above. It is important to plaster right up the wall to get a positive join between the parts of the mould.
3. Peel away the clay wall. If the mould has only two parts, apply soap, Vaseline or clay wash to the exposed plaster wall and make the second half of the mould. If there are more than two, build a clay wall to contain the next piece and apply release agent to the plaster wall of the first piece. Make the second piece. Continue like this until the mould is finished.

In the fence method, all the pieces of the mould are made at the same time:

1. Decide where the mould is to divide. Along the dividing lines, push in overlapping pieces of thin card or plastic, or pieces of thin brass sold for the purpose, to make a 'fence' 3 or

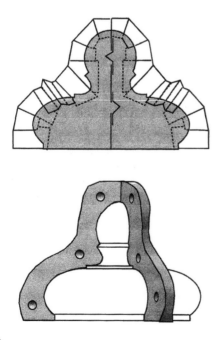

Dividing plaster moulds of more than one piece. Top: using brass or plastic shim pushed into the clay. The parts of the mould are made all at once; as the plaster goes off, it is scraped back to reveal the top of the shim (take care not to bridge the dividing lines with scrim). When set, the mould can be broken open along the shim line; small zigzags in the wall help to realign the mould. This method is most often used for waste moulds. Below: soft clay walls are used to define the sections of the mould, which are made one at a time. Shallow depressions are made in the wall for alignment. Set plaster must be soaped to prevent subsequent pieces from adhering. This method is much slower, but produces a more accurate, longer lasting mould.

4cm high between the parts. Slightly zigzagging lines will help the parts of the mould to register together later.

Clay original of a helmet ready for first half of mould to be made.

2. Make all the parts of the mould at once. Don't worry if plaster covers the fence in places, but try not to bridge it with scrim. If using brass fence, beware of cutting your hands on it.
3. As the plaster hardens, trim it away with a knife or rasp until you can see the top of the fence all the way along each dividing line.

Whichever technique you use, these moulds can be difficult to open, even when made from clay originals. Three measures can be taken to make this easier:

* Make sure the mould is strong enough to withstand the force involved in opening it, particularly the walls around the edge of each piece.
* In either technique, small wedge-shaped pieces of clay can be used to form openings between the pieces in which some kind of lever can be placed. In the clay wall technique, place them on the upper edge of the plaster walls before making the next piece of the mould. In the fence technique simply stick them to one side of the fence, near the top edge.
* Flooding water into the mould as you prise it open – either from a jug or straight from the tap – helps to break the bond between the mould and the original.

FLEXIBLE MOULDS

Fifty years ago, the only flexible mould-making materials were natural materials such as gelatin and latex. Both can still be used, but they are overshadowed by an array of superior synthetic materials, capable of reproducing great detail and coping with varying degrees of undercut.

Materials

RTV Silicone Rubber
The material of choice for flexible moulds and the most expensive. A syrupy liquid is mixed

with a small amount of a catalyst to initiate curing and the mixture is poured or spread over an original where it cures to a rubber-like consistency. Other additives may be used to change the viscosity of the uncured mixture or to accelerate the cure. A wide variety of products is available, of varying hardness. After its flexibility, the other great advantage of silicone rubber is that it is self-releasing. This means that, with most materials, no release agent is necessary either on the original from which the mould is being made or in the silicone-rubber mould when a cast is made in it.

Because of its high cost, silicone rubber is often used as a thin 'skin mould' backed by an outer shell of plaster or GRP; another common economy measure is to put unwanted moulds through a food processor and use the resulting 'meal' to bulk out fresh rubber. Fast-curing, non-toxic silicones are now available for use in life casting.

Polyurethane Rubber

Considerably cheaper than silicones, these materials also often have greater tear strength. Some have much lower viscosity, which helps to reduce air entrapment in poured moulds, and the 1:1 mix ratio of many of them is much easier to handle. They have a few disadvantages in comparison with silicones. Both the original (when making the mould) and the mould itself (when casting) need careful treatment with appropriate release agents. Like other urethanes, they are moisture-sensitive, and cannot be used to make moulds direct from wet modelling materials. Lastly, they tend to have short shelf lives.

Polysulphides

These are somewhere between urethanes and silicones in price, but less widely available. They can be used directly over wet clay. Most originals do not need a release agent, but moulds need to be treated before casting with many materials.

Hot-Melt Vinyls

When heated, these materials become liquid, and can be poured over the original to make a mould. Old moulds may be melted down and reused. Vinyls have a naturally greasy surface but still need a release agent with tenacious casting materials such as urethane or epoxy resin. Originals must be heat resistant and dry. There is a slight shrinkage on cooling. Skin or shell-moulds are difficult to make, effectively limiting vinyls to poured moulds.

Dental Alginate

Although most often used for life casting (*see* below), alginate is also useful when you need a temporary flexible mould very quickly. The moulds do not keep and the moisture in the cured mould may react with or inhibit some casting materials.

Types of Flexible Mould

The types of flexible mould vary greatly in their complexity and in the time it takes to make them, and it is important to select one that will do the required job without creating unnecessary work.

The simplest type is suitable for small, 'one-sided' originals that have a flat or open back or base. The object is fixed temporarily to a baseboard, any gaps between its edges and the board being filled with clay or wax. A containing wall is built around the object, using clay, plywood, lino, Lego bricks or whatever; care is taken to seal this to the baseboard. If necessary, the prepared enclosure is then sprayed with a release agent. Liquid silicone or urethane is then poured in until it covers the original. The result is a one-piece block mould in which either solid or hollow casts can be made with suitable materials.

A fully three-dimensional original, where all sides are to be reproduced, can sometimes be moulded by suspending it in the rubber so that it is completely immersed. When cured, the

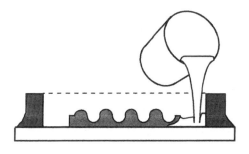

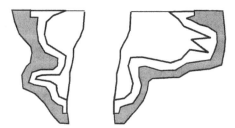

Release Agents

Release agents form a chemical or mechanical barrier that prevents the adhesion of a mould-making material to an original or a casting material to a mould. Often their use is not necessary – silicone rubber, for instance, releases from most originals and casting materials, while latex releases from plaster moulds. GRP materials or other composites containing adhesives being cast into rigid moulds are most likely to require a release agent; often a single layer of grease or wax is enough, though some situations, such as polyester casts from polyester moulds, demand complex, proprietary, release systems. Always experiment if you are unsure rather than risk spoiling the work.

ABOVE: Types of flexible mould. Block mould (top), poured into a 'containment field' built around the original with clay, wood or whatever. Very liquid mould rubber is an advantage, filling detail and allowing air bubbles to escape. A skin mould (bottom), made by spreading thixotropic rubber over the original in a layer 5 or 10mm thick, and then building a rigid outer case with plaster or GRP.

RIGHT: Block moulds of chandelier parts waiting to be poured.

Releasing a Kalashnikov magazine from a two-piece, silicone mould.

block of rubber is cut open with a scalpel far enough to release the original (and subsequent casts). An 'ingate' for the casting resin and any necessary risers to allow air bubbles to escape are carved into one of the cut surfaces.

Usually, though, three-dimensional objects will need a mould made in more than one piece. The simplest two-part block moulds are made by pouring a suitable depth of resin into an enclosure and suspending the original in it, up to the line where the mould is to divide. When this half of the mould has cured, several shallow, conical holes are cut in the surface of the rubber to align the two halves when casting, and a parting

agent is applied. The second half of the mould is poured. After curing, the two halves are separated and the original is removed. An ingate and risers can be cut into one side of the mould.

An alternative, useful when the dividing line between the two halves is not in one plane or when it is impracticable to suspend the original, is to embed it in clay or wax up to the desired dividing line. An enclosure is built around the clay bed and the first half poured. After curing, the half-made mould is inverted, the clay is removed, parting agent applied and the second half is poured as above.

Moulds in two or more pieces need some arrangement to hold them together against the pressure of liquid resin poured into them when casting. Sometimes this may be as simple as a few rubber bands around them, as with relatively chunky moulds made of firm rubber. Often, though, rubber bands alone will distort the mould and may not prevent leakage. The pressure must be more evenly distributed. Plywood backings for each half spread the pressure of rubber bands, ties or gentle clamping. Alternatively, if a suitable plastic or metal container is used for containment when the mould is made, it can be pushed back into this for casting.

Larger Work

Larger moulds require a completely different approach; the cost of the rubber usually prohibits the pouring of large blocks. Instead it is used to make a thin skin over the original, which is then supported by a rigid case of a cheaper material. Skin moulding also allows for much greater economy with small moulds.

There are two quite different ways to go about making skin moulds. The first, known as shell moulding, is derived from traditional gelatin moulding; it is by far the more laborious, but allows complete control over the thickness and exterior shape of the rubber skin. In this technique, soft modelling clay is used to create the desired shape of the rubber mould, in one or more parts. The rigid case or shell that will support the mould is made over this clay layer, usually in plaster or GRP. The cured case is lifted off, the clay is removed and the original is cleaned up; the case is treated with a release agent (if required) and carefully replaced. Liquid rubber compound is then poured into the cavity between the original and the case to create the skin. The time involved in making this type of mould – especially if it is in more than one piece – means that it is best used only when a long production run is required from the mould. Providing runners and risers, and getting the pieces of rubber skin and rigid case to re-register accurately, take a lot of planning.

The other skin-moulding technique is by far the more common in prop making. It uses thixotropic rubber to create the skin; the case is formed directly over this. With fewer steps, it is a much faster method, but there is less control over the thickness and form of the skin. Suitably thick rubber mould compounds are either thickened with an additive at the mixing stage or bought as a separate product. They are rarely truly thixotropic, retaining some tendency to flow under gravity. With urethanes, it is usually necessary to build the skin up in two or more layers, allowing each to part-cure before applying the next; the first should be brushed well into all the detail as air bubbles are more likely to be trapped under thickened rubber. Some silicones are thick enough to be applied as a single layer, if you are prepared to spend some time scooping up the rubber and putting it back where you want it. Urethanes have much better tear strength than silicones, which can be reinforced with open-weave fabrics if necessary.

Making a Silicone Rubber Skin Mould

1. Roll out some soft modelling clay and cut it into strips; use these to build a low wall around the original.

Making a silicone skin mould: a low clay wall placed around the original to create a strong, neat edge.

Starting to spread the silicone, using a wooden mixing stick as a spatula.

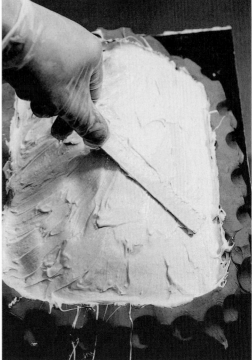

Smoothing off the rubber.

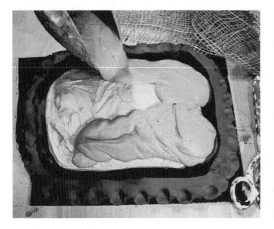

After the rubber has cured, the clay wall is moved further out and a batch of plaster is poured over the mould.

Scrim is immediately embedded in the wet plaster.

2. Mix up a quantity of silicone rubber with a catalyst and thixotropizing agent. Using a brush or spatula, spread rubber over the original and up the dividing wall. Try to avoid trapping air bubbles under the rubber and to keep the depth uniform right up to the edge. If necessary, add another layer when the first is still tacky. The thickness needed will depend on the size of the mould – in the example illustrated it is about 8mm.
3. Allow the rubber to cure. Pull the clay wall away, trim the ragged edge of rubber and replace the clay wall a few centimetres further out.
4. Apply a layer of neat plaster, right to the edge of the clay wall. Press pieces of scrim into it and fold overlaps back into the wet plaster to make a neat, strong edge. Smooth another layer of plaster over the top so that the scrim is completely invisible. When the plaster has gone off, remove the clay wall and tidy up the edge of the plaster with a knife or rasp.

Gelatin Mould Material

A cheap but useful flexible mould material can be made from glue size or pearl glue and cheap antifreeze. Soak the glue in plenty of cold water overnight. Pour off the water that has not been absorbed and heat the swollen glue in a double boiler. When it has melted, mix in a volume of antifreeze equal to the original volume of dry glue. Pour into moulds while still hot; on cooling it sets to a tough, slightly waxy-feeling jelly.

There are several limitations to this material. It is runny until it sets and so can be used only for block or shell moulds. It is used hot, which may affect certain originals. Most importantly, it melts again when heated, so casting materials that produce a lot of heat as they cure will destroy their moulds. Only one cast can be made from large moulds. Casts in small or shallow moulds produce less heat, and multiple casts in both polyester and urethane resins are

---

Flexible Mould Compounds: Health and Safety

Silicone, urethane and polysulphide compounds all involve hazardous chemicals. The diisocyanate hardeners supplied with most urethanes are particularly dangerous. Always read and follow the manufacturer's instructions and obtain material safety data sheets for each product. Always wear goggles and gloves when handling these products; avoid all skin contact as a matter of course. Do not eat or drink in your work area. Clean up carefully, and, if other people have access to your work area, place warning signs around uncured rubber.

---

possible, using a soft wax release agent. The shelf life of the mould is limited; storage in a plastic bag in a refrigerator can extend it.

LIFE CASTING

Life casting is the process of making moulds of parts of the body and casting from them. The most common application is probably mask-making, where a cast of an actor's face is used as a base for modelling to ensure a close fit. Sometimes hands, feet and faces may be cast and added to polystyrene work, removing the need to carve difficult and detailed parts. Occasionally, whole body casts are required.

Materials

The main requirements of mould-making materials for life casting are that they should be safe for the model and very fast setting. Several materials may be used.

Plaster Bandage

Plaster-impregnated bandage designed for setting broken bones can be used either as a mould

'Bronze' head of a youth, made from a life cast.

material in itself or as a rigid backing to flexible alginate moulds. It is the cheapest mould material and the easiest to use, but has severe limitations. It captures little fine detail unless it is carefully applied. Its rigidity rules out the moulding of undercuts, apart from slight ones around soft features such as nostrils. It also sticks to hair unless it is heavily greased; features such as bushy eyebrows may need to be completely caked with grease or masked with fine tissue paper. The skin needs only lightly greasing. Despite these limitations, plaster bandage remains an excellent material for quick, cheap life moulds and is particularly fast for large-scale work. As a support material for flexible moulds, it is useful for its lightness and speed of setting; avoiding undercuts is less of an issue and there is no need for large amounts of Vaseline.

To use plaster bandage, cut a supply of pieces before starting (do not tear it – the plaster will fall out). Float each piece on the surface of a wide bowl of warm water for a few seconds (immersing single pieces makes them too wet). Lift it out and run it through your fingers to spread the wet plaster evenly, then use it quickly, massaging it well into the skin and features of your model to avoid air bubbles. Work it well into the pieces it overlaps, to ensure a good join; if possible, never let an edge set before the overlapping piece is applied. A small mould like a face needs three or four layers of bandage, with strips of bandage gathered into a thicker rim around the edge. Heavier moulds can be made by wetting multiple layers of bandage; these may need to be immersed to get enough water into them. It is always best to work in a team, with one person wetting the bandage and one (or more) applying it.

Alginate
This is a mould material intended specifically for life casting. It comes as a fine powder (sometimes mint-flavoured because of its use in dentistry) and is mixed with water to form a thick liquid that sets in a few minutes to a dense but flexible 'jelly'. Alginate takes extremely fine detail and releases cleanly from skin and hair (although fine hair around the temples, for instance, can become caught in it with painful consequences). Moulds must be supported with some kind of rigid backing, usually made of plaster bandage. The alginate tears easily and must be handled carefully. Most importantly, it starts to dry out and shrink from the moment it is made; casts must be made within a few hours. Wrapping the mould in a damp cloth and a plastic bag and keeping it in the refrigerator prolongs its life for a couple of days.

The dampness of alginate moulds theoretically precludes the use of casting materials such as polyester and urethane resins that are inhibited by moisture, although some urethanes seem to cast quite happily in it. Epoxies, plaster and polymer plaster materials all cast well in these moulds.

To mix up alginate, weigh or measure out separate bowls of water and alginate according to the ratio recommended by the manufacturer. When you are ready for the mix, add the water to the alginate and mix briskly with a plastic spatula or wooden spoon, or with a mixing blade in a drill. Try not to trap air in the mix. Working with alginate is all about speed and timing – the material sets quickly, and a fresh mix won't then stick to it unless a bonding agent is applied. Intricate work is best done in a number of batches, all measured out before starting and mixed by an assistant as the work proceeds. Apply alginate with a wooden mixing stick or a wide plastic spatula. When working on vertical surfaces, be ready to keep putting it back where you want it – it sags and runs, especially when freshly mixed. Work to keep a good thickness – say 1cm – around the edge of a mould; feather edges tear easily and dry out particularly fast.

Silicone Rubber

Life moulding materials based on this are available: non-toxic, extremely fast-setting cousins to standard RTV silicones. However, currently these materials are very expensive and are used mainly by hi-tech specialist operators.

Making a Life Mould of a Face with Alginate and Plaster Bandage

Have ready before your model arrives:

* a comfortable chair with plenty of work area around it and a table for your materials;
* a towel to go round their neck and something to protect clothes; a hair band or swimming cap to keep hair out of the way;
* measured containers of alginate and water, and tools for mixing and applying it. Two batches, each making about 250g of mixed alginate are enough for a face, or three if the neck is to be included;
* ten or fifteen 25cm lengths of plaster bandage and a bowl for wetting them. Fill with hot water immediately before starting work so the plaster sets faster;
* 'straws' to go in the model's nostrils to enable them to breath. Make these by rolling up small squares of paper and sticking with tape. The diameter is important: they should fit securely without distorting the shape of the nose; 3 or 4cm is long enough;
* moisturizer or cold cream; they help alginate to release from dry skin;
* paper towels or similar for cleaning your hands.

As well as enabling things to run smoothly, preparation helps your subject to feel confident in you.

Explain what you are going to do, and how long each stage will take. Many people do not particularly enjoy having their faces cast and some are panicked by having their eyes or mouths covered. It is important to keep talking, particularly after the eyes are covered; describe what you are doing and where the alginate is going next. Arrange a code for basic yes or no communication. Make sure that your subject can breathe freely through the nose – if this is not possible, postpone the session for a couple of days.

Seat your model; drape their clothes and put a towel round the neck to catch drips. An upward-tilted face is easiest if you can arrange some sort of headrest. Test the straws for size and adjust if necessary. It is a great help if the model is willing to keep hold of them and insert them when the moment comes. Apply cream if it is to be used.

Mix a batch of alginate until all the lumps are gone and start to apply it. Work upwards, spreading a big helping up the jawline from the chin to the ear on either side, then fill in the cheeks to just below the eyes and on either side of the mouth and nose (you will have to keep returning to these areas to catch the alginate as it sags). Then, after telling the model, cover the mouth – place a spatula-load of alginate in the middle of the mouth and spread firmly each way into the corners to push out air bubbles. Make sure that the alginate covers the top lip right up to the base of the nose.

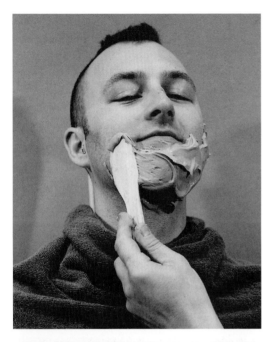

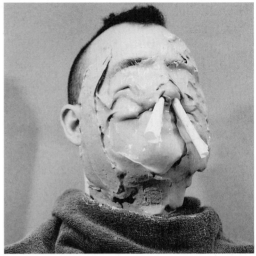

LEFT: Life casting a face: starting to spread alginate over the jaw.

ABOVE: After covering the upper lip, the straws are put in place and the alginate layer continues.

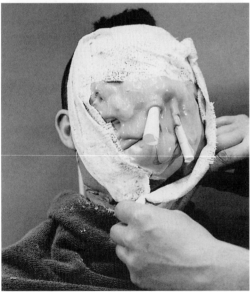

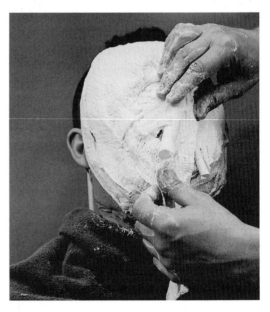

When the alginate layer is complete, it is immediately covered with several layers of plaster bandage, starting at the edges to give them plenty of time to go off.

Finishing the plaster bandage.

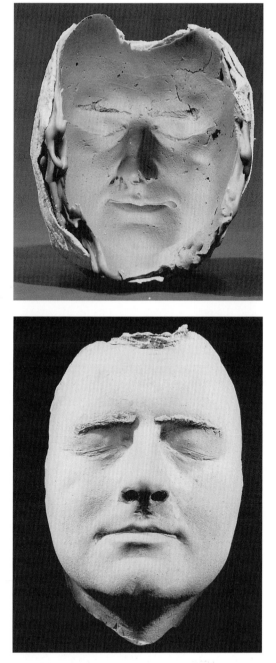

TOP: *The mould...*
BOTTOM: *...and its cast.*

Get your assistant to start mixing the next batch around now. If you know how long the mixing and setting each take, you can time exactly when to do this. Now put in the straws (if in place from the start they prevent you from covering the mouth properly). If possible, get your model to do this – their hands should still be clean. Then immediately cover the nose, working the alginate carefully around the nostrils and straws; a smaller tool such as the handle of a plastic teaspoon is useful for this.

Switch to the new batch of mixture if you have not yet done so, and spread an extra layer around the edge of the mould at the jawline. Then, after a suitable warning, cover each eye in turn. Use plenty of alginate and don't be scared to be firm – you need to be to avoid trapping air in the inside corners. Use the remaining alginate to cover the forehead, aiming for a thick edge, and to build up the mould anywhere you think that it is too thin.

As soon as you are sure that the alginate is not sagging, start to cover the mould with plaster bandage. As with the alginate, strong edges are vital; they have to be able to withstand the stress of removing the mould as soon as the plaster has gone off. Do not try to cover every single patch of alginate, particularly around the nose – it takes too long and the point of the plaster bandage is to cradle the alginate to retain its proper shape. Three or four layers should be enough, with extra reinforcement around the edges. When it is done, wet one final piece of bandage and leave it on the rim of the bowl to tell you when the plaster has all gone off.

Relax for two or three minutes as you wait for the plaster to set. Keep talking to your model, who is now at the height of sensory deprivation. When you think the plaster is strong enough, start to remove the mould. Get rid of the straws first with a quick downward tug on each. Then ask the subject to start to move, or try to move, the facial muscles to help to break the vacuum. At the same time, pull at the mould near the ears; it should come away easily, pivoting down to help to free the nose. The only thing that may hold up removal of an alginate mould is hair trapped in it, usually around the hairline and at the temples; release the mould slowly and gently by working your fingers down behind it at the trouble spots, and use more cream or Vaseline next time. Thick, bristly hair (such as a moustache) is less of a problem.

Cast from the mould immediately, or wrap it in polythene to delay drying. The holes left by the straws can be blocked with pellets of plaster bandage.

Large Life Moulds

Particular problems arise when making a life mould on a larger scale, such as a torso or whole body. First, it takes longer to cover the area and the weight of the mould is greater, so a greater degree of stamina and commitment is demanded of the model. Secondly, the mould will probably

need to be in two or more parts and a way must be found to make strong, registered interfaces between these parts quickly. Lastly, while plaster bandage is sturdy enough in small, strongly three-dimensional shapes, such as face moulds, large areas of more gentle curvature are flimsy. They need careful reinforcement with timber even to survive the removal process.

The use of alginate for large moulds is impractical for all but the most well-supported poses because of its weight and the extra time involved in making it. Any kind of dynamic pose is best moulded in plaster bandage alone (using plenty of Vaseline or baby oil as a release agent). Even then, ways of supporting the model should be carefully thought out. One of the consequences of holding a pose while warm bandage is applied seems to be gradual loss of awareness of the muscle tension required to hold the pose, with models tensing up severely, getting cramp or relaxing to the point that they

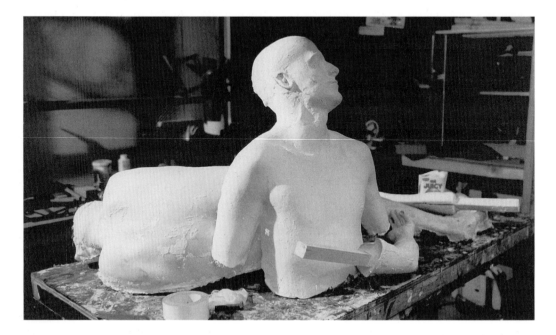

Life-casts awaiting finishing.

fall over. The speed with which the mould can be made becomes crucial, and the key is efficient teamwork. Two teams of two, with a fifth person as a floating troubleshooter, is the ideal set-up. Other practical requirements are a warm, private workspace with plenty of room and a castored work table for each team's materials. Arrangements for supporting the model in the required pose may vary from a fixed, vertical, scaffolding pole to which horizontal pieces can be attached at desired heights, to a padded ply board that can be inclined at different angles.

Models can be cast naked, using Vaseline or a soft white paraffin/mineral oil mix as a release, or clothed, in which case the clothes need to be suitably greased and the extra weight of them borne in mind. Before preparing the model, however, it is essential to rehearse the pose, in order to plan the division of the mould and the means of support. The wooden reinforcement can also be designed once the division has been decided; cut pieces of wood to suit each part of the mould, taping them to the model to ensure that they fit and meet each other as planned, then put them to one side.

The division of the mould should be planned not only to avoid undercuts (although the flexibility of most parts of the body gives you some leeway), but also to avoid awkwardly shaped pieces and to facilitate the subsequent casting process. Once the materials and model have been prepared, the divisions can be drawn on direct using greasepaint or lipstick and the order of the work decided.

The plaster bandage can be applied several layers at a time, in quite large pieces. Work begins along the division lines. Lengths of bandage three or four layers thick are wetted and then partially gathered concertina-fashion along their length and placed along one side of each division line. Once in situ they can be moulded in to a wall or flange shape of roughly triangular section by running the fingers along them. A blunt, polished tool helps to form the face that will meet the adjacent piece of mould. A margin of thinner bandage must be left extending into the part of the mould to which the wall belongs to overlap with other bandage. As soon as the wall of the first piece starts to set, it is brushed with oil or soap and a matching wall for the adjacent piece of the mould formed up against it, ensuring that no bandage crosses the line.

This technique has several advantages over the old method – covering the model all over with bandage and then cutting the mould up with scissors – that outweigh its being slightly slower. First, the edges produced are far stronger; secondly, they mate with each other when the mould is reassembled; and thirdly, no sharpened steel blades are involved.

At the same time as the walls for a section of mould are being made, its interior should be filled in – plaster bandage bonds far better to unset than to set material. As each section is completed, its wooden reinforcement is added, using plenty of bandage to lash it together and to attach it to the mould itself; 1in × 1in or 2cm square sections are ample for most moulds. It is also possible to build in reinforcement by using paper rope and bandage to form ribs, although the strength of these is not comparable with that of wood.

When the mould is removed, the parts should separate easily along the division lines. If there are problems, look for stray overlaps of bandage or insert a blunt knife blade between the two walls and gently prise them apart; they should be strong enough to undergo this.

Even if the head is to be involved in the final cast, it is best to mould it separately if the area of the body involved goes much below the shoulders. When making the body section, mould up to and on to the jawline. Then make a separate mould of the head (in similar pose). When the body section has been cast, the head mould may be registered into it using the hard jawline and filled in situ.

6 CASTING AND LAMINATING

'Casting' means placing material in a mould and allowing it to set into a 'cast' of the mould. 'Laminating' here means combining a glue or resin with some kind of fibrous reinforcement to produce a composite material, either in a

LEFT: Miniature cast of a performer's face. The original alginate mould was allowed to shrink over several days; a cast was then taken from it and a second alginate mould made. This was also allowed to shrink, until the desired size was reached; an epoxy/glass cast was then taken and used to make the prop. Smoke, GSMD; designer: Dora Schweitzer; photograph: Lawrence Burns.

mould or over a core of some other material. While not all casts are laminated and not all laminates are made in moulds, the two share many materials and techniques and are so closely related that it is hard to tell where one stops and the other begins. It therefore makes sense to deal with them together.

MATERIALS

Materials for casting and laminating divide into these basic groups:

✳ glass reinforced plastic (GRP) laminates, combinations of glass-fibre reinforcement with synthetic resins that set after the addition of a

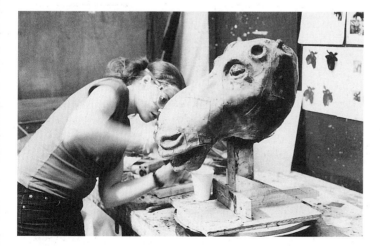

Laminating epoxy and glass cloth straight over a clay original. The clay was removed (with some difficulty) through a hole in the neck and the GRP shell then slipped off the armature.

An elliptical dome cast in clear urethane resin in a plaster waste mould. Polishing the extremely tough urethane took many hours, but it was felt that polyester would have been too fragile. The Snowmaiden, GSMD; *designer: Isabella Bywater; photograph: Laurence Burns.*

catalyst or hardener; these are important prop-making materials;

* resin/filler mixtures that can be poured or pasted into moulds to produce small casts or modelled over laminates;
* plaster-based materials, either poured or laminated with glass or natural fibre reinforcement;
* 'low-tech' composites such as papier mâché.

There are also a few stragglers – mostly proprietary materials borrowed from other industries.

GRP

Made by sticking together glass fibres with a synthetic resin, GRP combines the adhesive power of the resin (which on its own sets hard but is brittle) with the tensile strength of the glass reinforcement to produce a strong, lightweight material that can be formed into complex shapes. It has many uses, from the making of surf boards, boats and vehicle bodywork, to props, sculpture and display work. The fact that much of this work is carried out on an amateur or very light industrial basis has led to the development of products and processes that are suitable for small-scale use with minimal equipment.

GRP materials have many applications in theatre prop making, ranging from small casting jobs to the covering of masonry, sculptural or landscape elements and the making of armour. They cast well into silicone rubber moulds and plaster waste moulds, can be filled either case, layers of glass reinforcement are added until the desired strength is reached, sometimes separated by layers of filled resin or core material to increase stiffness.

Glass Reinforcement

Glass fibres for GRP reinforcement are very thin – in the region of 0.01mm – and are gathered into bundles of several dozen fibres for processing into the many sheet forms available to the end user.

Two common sheet forms are of everyday use to prop makers: 'chopped strand mat' (CSM) and glass cloth. CSM is made by cutting the strands into approximately 50mm lengths that are then bonded together into a randomly arranged 'mat'. In use, a solvent in the resin dissolves the binder holding the mat together, and rolling or stippling then separates the fibres and spreads them out in the wet resin. A range of thicknesses is available, described by weight per unit area. Lightweight CSM (for instance, 300g/sq m) conforms most easily to complex three-dimensional shapes, while heavier grades (600 or 900g/sq m) work best on plain areas, and will not work easily into detail nor over sharp corners. Each layer of CSM requires around twice its own weight of resin.

Glass cloth is made from continuous strands in a wide variety of weights and weaves. Plain and twill weave cloths in light and medium weights (135–200g/sq m) are most useful. Plain weave cloth is also available in tape form, in a variety of widths. Cloth can be more difficult to 'wet out' than CSM, particularly when it is tightly woven, but requires less resin – roughly its own weight – which makes for a stronger laminate. The fibres move about less during laminating, making even thicknesses and surfaces easier to produce.

Two other sheet materials that may be useful are 'surface mat' and 'surfacing tissue'. These are very lightweight products not really intended for structural use, but in delicate work or for some polystyrene-covering jobs they may be all that is required.

Tinted clear polyester chandelier drops being released from a mould.

with metal or mineral powders and polished to resemble other materials, and can be used over polystyrene or clay work.

The essential process (there are many variations) involves the mixing of liquid resin with a catalyst or hardener, and using this mixture to 'wet out' or saturate layers of matted or woven glass fibre. This is done either in a mould or over some kind of core or 'plug' which may be removed when the GRP has hardened, or simply left in place. Moulds are first given a layer of coloured, filled or thickened resin (a 'gel coat'), which becomes the outside surface of the cast; when covering plugs, a final layer of similar resin (a 'top coat') has the same function. In

GRP reinforcements. Top: glass cloth and chopped strands. Bottom: chopped strand mat and coremat.

Glass is also available as loose, chopped strands about 6 mm long, and as milled fibres about 1mm long. Both products may be mixed direct with resin to produce a paste of fair structural strength that can be spread into a mould or over a core.

Polyester Resin

This is the standard material for GRP laminates and may also be used without reinforcement for small casts or cavity mouldings (*see* below). It is cheap, readily available and easy to use. It contains styrene monomer, which is given off as a harmful vapour until the resin has set. It must be used with proper ventilation – ideally enclosure and extraction, or outdoors. Occasional small-scale work may be done in large, airy workspaces with a respirator fitted with an organic-vapour filter, provided that this does not endanger others.

One of the functions of the styrene is to dissolve the binder that holds chopped strand mat together, releasing the individual fibres and allowing the reinforcement to drape over three-dimensional shapes. It also dissolves both expanded and extruded polystyrene on contact, requiring that the polystyrene is completely sealed, either by several coats of paint or by a layer of aluminium foil. Despite this and the health hazards associated with styrene vapour, many prop makers prefer it to epoxy – it is only a fraction of the price and its compatibility with CSM makes it faster and easier to use.

The setting of polyester resin is initiated by adding a small percentage of a catalyst – usually methyl ethyl ketone peroxide. The setting time varies with the proportion of catalyst – from 0.5 to 3 per cent – but also depends on the amount of another additive, the 'accelerator', in the resin. This reacts with the catalyst, causing heat to build up; the more accelerator, the more heat is generated. Unaccelerated resins can set only if heat is applied externally. Most resins in the DIY sector are pre-accelerated, the amount of accelerator determining the intended use; resins to be spread out in thin layers need more than those for casting large volumes. Do not get them mixed up. If you do buy accelerator separately, make sure that it is always thoroughly mixed into the resin before the catalyst is added and that neat accelerator and catalyst never come into contact with one another.

Laminating resin comes as a clear or slightly tinted syrupy liquid; fire-retardant products may be whitish and opaque. Gel coat resins are similar in colour and more thixotropic – they flow when you apply pressure with a mixing stick or brush, but not otherwise (like mayonnaise). Most resins set with a tacky surface where they have been exposed to the air; top-coat resin contains wax to overcome this and is slightly thickened. Casting resins contain less accelerator to allow for the greater build-up of heat in deep moulds.

Rather than buy resins formulated for different applications, it is quite possible to use a 'general purpose' resin, adding fumed silica to thicken it and a solution of wax in styrene to reduce surface tack. This may be more convenient or economical for small-scale operations, although these mixtures are unlikely to perform as well as formulated products.

Epoxy Resin

At around four times the price of polyester, epoxy is much stronger, producing tougher, lighter laminates. It forms powerful bonds with other materials and hardware items and can be mixed with fillers such as colloidal silica, talc or marble dust to a consistency that can be modelled

Part of a cauldron cast in epoxy GRP, with a mixture of graphite and aluminium powder in the gel coat. Polished up with steel wool to a deep metallic finish.

over the basic glass laminate. Its cost makes it less likely to be used for solid casts.

Epoxy is supplied as a two-part system; 'resin' and 'hardener' components are mixed at fixed ratios such as 3:1 or 5:1. The ratio cannot be varied and some manufacturers offer slow and fast hardeners to meet the need for different setting times. Some also supply pumps that attach to their containers and dispense resin and hardener in the prescribed ratio – these are essential when many small batches are being mixed.

The hardeners in particular present considerable health hazards: they are corrosive and toxic by skin contact, which should be completely avoided. Vapour from the curing resin can be harmful by inhalation. Small-scale work can be carried out in a large, open workshop with a good through draught (assisted, if necessary); larger work may need local exhaust ventilation.

Epoxy resins cannot dissolve the binder in standard chopped strand mat and are used with woven glass cloth, which is significantly more expensive than CSM. Mixing epoxy with loose, chopped strands makes a paste that naturally 'mats' into thin layers as it is applied to the work, but the resulting laminate is not as strong as one made with cloth.

Fillers and Pigments

Fillers are powders that are added to a resin to thicken it, to change its appearance or to give it some specific property, such as fire-retardance. Low-cost fillers are mostly quarry products: talc, calcium sulphate (gypsum), china clay powder, slate powder and marble dust are all used, either to make resin pastes and putties for texturing, detailing and 'fairing' (smoothing uneven surfaces), or for their colour. The denser fillers such as slate and marble improve chip resistance in areas of fine detail, and all these fillers help to minimize cracking in solid castings by reducing shrinkage. Talc and clay pastes may be used in the middle of 'sandwich' laminates, thickening them for greater rigidity without adding more glass. Most of these fillers contain free silicates that are harmful by inhalation.

Fumed silica (also known as colloidal silica, and by trade names such as Cab-o-sil) is a very useful thickening agent that can make a resin completely thixotropic while adding very little weight. These mixtures are less sticky, dragging less on tools than those made with other fillers. They can also stick to silicone rubber moulds, unless a suitable silicone-free release agent is used. Fumed silica is amorphous silicon dioxide and, although it doesn't present the same hazards associated with it as crystalline silica, is very light and easily becomes airborne; take care not to inhale it. Other lightweight fillers include glass microspheres (tiny bubbles of glass sold under several trade names), which provide a low-strength paste that is easily sanded.

Powdered metals such as brass, copper and aluminium can be added to a gel coat or top coat and brought to a high polish after curing with steel wool, wet and dry paper and metal polish. They can be mixed for intermediate colours or modified with pigments or graphite powder. High ratios of filler to resin – at least equal parts by volume – are needed for good results; mixtures based on laminating resin are thick enough for use as gel coats. With polyester, the percentage of catalyst will need to be increased (check with the resin supplier).

A wide range of pigment pastes, both opaque and translucent, is available for colouring polyester resin, with a more restricted choice for epoxy. These are highly pigmented resin pastes that are added to the mix in small quantities; they are formulated for stability and easy mixing. Ordinary dry powder pigments may also be used, although the chemical content of them is not always predictable, as well as substances such as mica, 'pearl' pigments, glitter and bronze powders. Keeping pigment to resin ratios to a maximum of 10 per cent by weight helps to limit any interference with curing.

Core Materials

Thin laminates are naturally very flexible and often need to be made more rigid. One way to do this is to make the laminate thicker by bulking it out with a 'core' layer between two layers of reinforcement. This can be done with a resin/filler paste, although these are heavy and a uniform layer may be hard to achieve. A lighter and more reliable solution is to use a sheet material. Thin polyurethane foam makes a very light core, although it is difficult to use on complex shapes; the several brands of 'core matting', a felt-like sheet material, drape more easily. These products are particularly useful in making objects such as armour, where lightweight, rigid casts of uniform thickness are needed. There is a choice of products on the market, the more expensive offering better drape, lighter weight and a range of thicknesses.

Tools, Equipment and Other Materials

Apart from fume extraction, little expensive equipment is required. Protective equipment for either type of resin includes goggles, overalls and gloves (disposable vinyl for small-scale work; long nitrile for larger work); a respirator may be needed for polyester resin and dust masks used when handling fillers. The use of a barrier cream helps to protect exposed skin, although any skin contact with resins, catalysts or hardeners should still be scrupulously avoided.

Small quantities of catalyst may be measured out with a plastic syringe, although the catalyst dispensers available from resin suppliers are much more convenient. Wooden mixing sticks can be made or bought; epoxies can be mixed with plastic teaspoons (polyester dissolves them). Flexible plastic mixing vessels allow cured resin to be broken out straight into the bin – plastic buckets will do for large quantities, and resin suppliers or decorators' merchants sell smaller pots. For small quantities, some kind of disposable pot may be more convenient. Waxed paper cups, if you can find them, will do for either type of resin; polystyrene cups may be used for epoxy. Food containers such as yoghurt cartons can be recycled, although many are no good for polyester resin.

'Laminating brushes', with plastic or unvarnished wooden handles, are available from resin suppliers and are cheap enough to be considered disposable when used with epoxy resin, which is difficult to wash off without large amounts of acetone. With practice, a lot of epoxy work can be carried out with disposable mixing sticks instead of brushes. Uncured polyester resin can be washed out, either with acetone, if the brush is needed quickly, or else with lots of cheap washing-up liquid and a rinse in warm water. In any case, the life of the brush will be short.

Workshops producing items such as boats or baths use ridged metal rollers to spread out and consolidate glass matting and remove air bubbles. Stronger laminates result, although the rollers need careful maintenance.

Other necessary equipment includes a knife, scissors or a disc cutter for cutting up glass reinforcement, strong craft scissors for cutting partly cured laminates, and a hacksaw for trimming cured work. Cured laminates can also be cut with a small angle grinder fitted with a cutting disc and shaped with a power sander; a dust mask should be worn for either process, and, if possible, the dust produced should be extracted at source.

Casting Polyester GRP in a Plaster Waste Mould

1. Make sure the mould is dry; apply a release agent, either a water-based film-forming product or a soft wax.
2. Catalyse some gel coat resin, mixing in pigment if required, and brush into the mould. Some gel coat resins aren't suitable for use with metal powders – if using these, mix with ordinary laminating resin instead. Allow to gel.
3. Catalyse laminating resin; if required, mix some with talc and fillet sharp corners. Press pieces of torn glass mat into tacky gel coat; paint with laminating resin. Continue to work with brush or roller until the glass binder dissolves and the glass 'wets out', becoming transparent. Add more layers as required. Core layers and additional glass can be added for thicker sandwich constructions.
4. Paint on a flow coat (laminating resin with pigment and a little silica) to smooth the rear surface, or spread it with heavily thickened paste and cover sheet plastic such as polypropylene to obtain a very smooth finish.
5. Wash tools in a hot water/washing-up liquid mix, or acetone if needed again immediately.

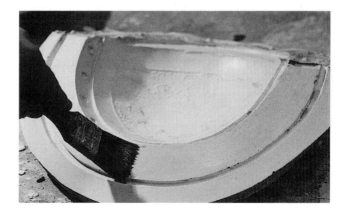

Casting polyester in a plaster waste mould. Painting the mould with parting agent – here a film-forming product based on sodium alginate.

Breaking away the mould with the aid of running water.

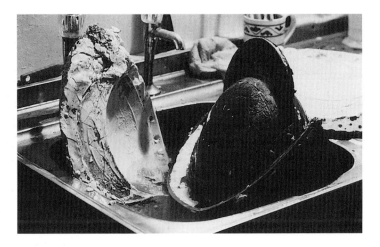

6. When the resin is cured, trim away excess of glass with scissors, grinder or sander. Break the mould away from the cast, using water to help them to separate and to remove the parting film from the cast.

Casting Epoxy and Chopped Glass in a Silicone Mould

This process differs from laying up glass and polyester in that the resin and glass are mixed together to form a paste and then applied to the mould.

A sort of gel coat – slightly thickened resin with pigment if required – should be used to pick up the detail of the mould and prevent the reinforcement from showing through. Then mix resin and hardener, and add pigment if required. Start to mix chopped strands into the resin. Keep adding them until the mixture starts to form soggy, wafer-like mats on the end of the mixing stick. There should be just enough resin in the mix to hold all the glass together; too much and it will drain into the low points in the mould, too little and the glass

Casting epoxy and chopped glass in a silicone mould. Brushing in a pigmented layer thickened with silica.

112

Painting in the gel coat: laminating resin filled with aluminium powder and black pigment.

Wetting out precut pieces of chopped strand mat.

BELOW: *Spreading metal-filled resin thickened with colloidal silica onto the exposed brim areas...*

...and covering with polypropylene sheet to produce a smooth surface.

Health and Safety

- Always read and follow the manufacturer's health and safety advice for any product. Obtain and read the Material Safety Data Sheet for every product you use. Keep them safely where they can be found in case there is an accident.
- Avoid skin contact with any resin or hardener products. Epoxy hardeners, polyester catalysts and urethane components containing isocyanates are particularly dangerous and you should devise methods of work that ensure protection from them. Wear goggles and disposable gloves when handling any of these products. Remember too that there is a danger from things such as contaminated gloves and spillage on the sides of containers, as well as from the work itself.
- Polyester resin emits toxic styrene vapour. The level considered safe is only just above the threshold at which the smell is detectable, so if you can smell the vapour strongly you are probably putting yourself at risk. If possible, use a low-emission resin. Always work in a well-ventilated area; if possible, use local exhaust ventilation with a positive supply of fresh air, otherwise wear a respirator with an organic vapour cartridge.
- The polyester catalyst methyl ethyl ketone peroxide (MEKP) is highly corrosive and can cause severe burns; avoid all skin contact and avoid breathing its vapour.
- Epoxy resin, hardener and mixtures of the two can cause dermatitis and sensitization to other chemicals; the hardener may also be corrosive. Avoid all skin contact. Avoid breathing epoxy vapour.

- One component of most urethane resin products contains isocyanate compounds that are toxic in minute quantities. Mix and pour urethanes slowly and carefully; do not do anything that might cause splashes. Always wear goggles and gloves and avoid breathing the vapour. Throw away clothing or equipment contaminated with the isocyanate component. Avoid breathing vapour.
- All these resins are exothermic (produce heat) as they cure. Most are intended to be used in thin layers, and large amounts left in mixing pots may overheat, producing toxic fumes and even fire. If this starts to happen, cover the mixing pot with cold water and take it outside. Mix only the amount of resin you need; if you do end up with an excess, spread it out thinly to cure. Different hardeners or suitably low catalyst ratios should be used for bulky castings.
- Most fillers are fine powders; many contain crystalline silicates and some are light enough to become easily airborne. Wear goggles and a suitable dust mask when handling any fillers in case of spillage. Close containers immediately after use.
- Strands of glass protruding from cured laminates are as sharp as needles. If there is any chance of the back of a laminate being handled, finish it with a thick flowcoat or a layer of lightweight cloth. Wear suitable gloves when removing untrimmed laminates from moulds; trim them as soon as possible.
- When sanding, grinding or machining cured laminates or resin castings, wear a suitable dust mask and protect your skin from contact with dust. Dust from freshly cured resins may still contain toxic compounds.

Applying the chopped strand/epoxy mixture with a wooden spatula. The tendency of this mixture to form thin layers makes it very quick to use.

BELOW: The finished cast. Note the needles of epoxy/ glass at bottom right; these need to be removed as soon as possible after curing. The cast should be handled with gloves until this has been done.

will be fluffy and unmanageable. When the mix is right, start to lay it into the mould; with the right consistency this is quite a quick process.

The mix forms layers easily that can be distributed round the mould. The trick is to get even coverage – using a different pigment from that in the gel coat helps. The cured spikes of glass are razor-sharp – this is not a process for making masks that will be worn – and need to be removed with a file or belt sander before the cast may be handled safely without gloves.

OTHER MATERIALS

Urethanes

These products come as two or more parts which, after mixing, either set solid or expand into a foam. The former are the material of choice for small, solid castings where intricacy or speed are important. They have many uses in industry, so there are many on the market: clear, opaque, fast, slow and so on; they are primarily intended for casting, not laminating. There are several advantages over polyester and epoxy:

* Greater toughness: they may be dropped or drilled with less risk of damage.
* Very fast-curing versions are available.
* They are very runny; intricate moulds can be filled quickly and air bubbles are less likely to be trapped in the cast.

115

* Mixing is simple, often a 1:1 ratio.
* They take metal powders well, polishing easily to a high finish.

These materials usually contain highly toxic isocyanates (*see* the health and safety guidance on page 114). Other disadvantages are:

* They are expensive.
* They have a short shelf life after their containers are opened; some manufacturers offer an inert gas 'blanket' that is sprayed into part-used bottles before storage, which extends the shelf life.
* Some products are difficult to buff up to a high polish because of their inherent toughness.
* Like polyester, their cure is inhibited by moisture, although they can be cast in damp moulds (alginate or clay, for instance) if a slight loss of surface finish is acceptable.
* Like epoxy, they are aggressively adhesive and are best cast in silicone rubber moulds; anything else needs careful treatment with appropriate release agents – manufacturers will recommend and in some cases sell these.

Urethane foams vary from rigid to very soft and flexible. Rigid foams have many uses, from back-filling vacuum-formed mouldings to casting 'blanks' to carve or turn; the soft foams are useful for puppets and prosthetics, and for casts that must subsequently be bent around other forms.

The expansion of both types of foam is uncontrollable without the use of some kind of mould. Repeatable casts are best made in silicone rubber moulds, but simple shapes will even release from suitably prepared plaster moulds. Whatever the mould, the best results are achieved by placing a measured amount of mix in the mould and sealing or closing it securely before foaming starts (with most products, you have about one minute in which to do this). The mould needs to be strong and rigid to withstand the pressure of the foam – flexible moulds must be fully backed with plaster or GRP. The quantity of mix should be that which would fill the mould and about a quarter as much again if left to expand freely – start with too little and work up.

Simple shuttering to cast blanks for carving and turning can be made from plywood (for flat surfaces) or vinyl flooring (for curves). All surfaces must be thoroughly greased. Cylindrical moulds for lathe blanks involve simply holding a roll of the vinyl at the right diameter with a couple of loops of string. Stand the roll on a greased board and weight it down.

Turning and carving rigid urethane foam is similar to working with polystyrene, although the urethane is much tougher. Great care should be taken to contain the dust produced by turning, sawing and sanding: it is very fine and irritating and may contain toxic compounds.

Plaster-Based Materials

Traditional plaster casts are rarely used on stage because of their weight and fragility (if brittleness is what you want, *see* the section on breakaway items on page 121). If these limitations are acceptable, thin casts with fibrous reinforcement made in the same manner as plaster moulds are a cheap option. Work of any size will need a steel or timber structure built into the back of it.

The demand for tougher and more weatherproof plaster-based materials has led to the development of polymer solutions that are used in place of plain water. The resulting 'polymer plaster' is much stronger than traditional plaster and is acceptable for stage use both for poured casts of small, solid objects and as a glass-reinforced laminate. The latter has none of the flexibility of GRP and does not approach its strength to weight ratio, so that it should not be thought of as a water-based substitute, but as a useful alternative when weight is not critical.

Polymer plaster materials are available as complete systems, or the liquid polymer alone can be bought and mixed with any 'alpha gypsum' plaster. The latter is by far the cheaper option, although the convenience of a system that offers many ancillary products as well may make up for the premium you pay for the plaster.

Polymer plasters can be retarded with trisodium citrate and thickened with colloidal silica or proprietary thickeners. They may be coloured with dry pigments or with special pastes, modelled or textured before setting (if suitably filled and retarded) and sanded or otherwise machined afterwards.

As a casting material, polymer plaster releases from most flexible mould materials without a release agent. From plaster waste moulds, a layer of soft wax is enough. Laminates can be reinforced with conventional plasterer's scrim or multiaxial open-weave glass cloth; for extra strength sandwich two layers of glass around a filled core layer.

Laminates can be used to cover polystyrene work and can be overmodelled with polymer plaster thickened with colloidal silica or dry paper pulp. The use of talc during the modelling process prevents sticky hands and tools and helps to produce smooth, shiny surfaces.

Absorption Casting: Latex and Neoprene

Absorption casting is similar to the slip-casting process used in ceramics and uses specially formulated natural latex or synthetic compounds. The process requires a clean, unsealed plaster mould. The liquid casting material is poured in to fill the mould to the brim; left to stand, the mould absorbs moisture from it and a dense deposit of the casting material forms against the mould surface. The remainder is poured back into its container for later use and the deposit covering the walls of the mould is left to dry. The natural latex-based material is tough and flexible when dry, can take great detail and undercutting, but shrinks a great

deal. It is heavy, tending to sag under its own weight. The synthetic materials produce thinner, more rigid casts, still with some shrinkage and are less readily available.

Keep in mind the following when making moulds for this process:

* Vaseline or soft wax release agents on originals at the mould-making stage can migrate to the plaster mould surface and prevent it from absorbing evenly or at all; soap release agents do not affect the porosity of the plaster.
* With natural latex, dryness is not essential and fresh moulds can be used if necessary; the absorption stage simply takes longer.
* Moulds of uniform wall thickness produce the most uniform casts.

Making a Cast with Slush-Moulding Latex

Make sure that the mould is clean and will not leak. Set it so that it is firmly supported with the top edge level; prop up irregular moulds with wedges of fresh clay. Wearing goggles, mix the latex thoroughly in the tin and pour carefully into the mould. Just before the mould is completely full, you can adjust the levelling if necessary, using the latex as a guide. Stop any leaks with wet clay.

Leave the filled mould for a time so that a wall of latex can build up. As moisture is absorbed by the mould, the level of the latex drops slightly, and you should see the thickness of the wall.

When the latex deposit has built up to the thickness you want, pour the latex back into the tin. This is potentially the messiest part of the process; wear goggles, choose the point on the mould's edge most likely to pour well and pour in one swift, bold movement. Leave the mould propped up on the tin for a while so that the last of the latex can drain out, otherwise you will get a puddle of latex at the deepest point of the mould. Do not touch the deposit of latex on the mould surface. Leave the mould

somewhere warm overnight (or longer for a thick cast) to dry out. To test for dryness, press the latex near the bottom of the mould. It should be firm; any softness indicates wet latex beneath the dry skin.

When it is completely dry, dust the inside of the cast with talc (fresh latex surfaces may stick to each other) and pull out of the mould. Provided that the cast is fully dried it will withstand a lot of tugging to get it out of undercuts.

Papier Mâché

This can mean either a laminate made by gluing together pieces of torn paper, or a dough-like mixture of paper pulp and glue. Both can be used in moulds or over some kind of former.

Laminated paper is cheap and quick to make, although drying times may be a problem, particularly with thicker laminates cast in moulds. Lightweight paper laminates are delicate but remain an important mask-making material (a mask is relatively easy to protect from rough treatment). They can be laid up straight over a clay original; seal it with shellac or cling film or leave it to go leather-hard to speed drying. Stronger, heavier paper laminates can be used to make larger objects – sugar paper, thick brown paper or printmaker's blotting paper all work well. Any water-based glue will probably work; a mixture of strong size and wallpaper paste is cheap, easy to use and particularly tough.

Paper pulp mixtures are much stronger than laminates, but involve more preparation and a longer drying time. They are good for small castings or for taking up detail in larger moulds before backing with paper laminate. Pulp can be bought dry in sacks, or you can make it yourself (*see* the section on making paper pulp in the chapter on modelling).

Paper-based casting materials shrink as they dry, a solid pulp casting far more than a laminate where each layer is dried before the next is applied. Some laminating techniques use no glue in the first layer and will release from untreated plaster moulds. Other paper-based casts should be made in sealed and oiled plaster moulds or very firm silicone rubber moulds.

Celastic

Once a brand name and now a generic term for a composite casting material that consists of a felt-like fabric impregnated with cellulose cement. Dipping it in acetone or cellulose thinners softens it, enabling it to be cast into a mould or worked over clay. It dries quickly to a tough, lightweight shell. At one time it was the material of choice of many puppet and mask makers but its popularity has waned because of the solvent involved and it is now more difficult to obtain.

Thermoplastics

The term is used to describe synthetic polymers which, when heated, become soft enough to be formed into a new shape into which they 'set' as they cool. Industry employs a large number of these plastics for mass production. Nearly all (there is one notable exception) soften at temperatures too high for them to be handled, which limits their usefulness in prop making to 'hands-off' processes such as vacuum forming. Most plastics have a technical name (such as polyamide), an abbreviation of this (PA) and one or more common names or trade names (Nylon). You may find any of these being used.

Polycaprolactone (PCL)

This remarkable material can be worked comfortably with bare hands. It softens at just below 100°C, remains malleable for several minutes as it cools down, and sets to a tough, resilient state that can be carved or drilled. It can be softened again by reheating, is non-toxic and is biodegradable. Although caprolactones have been manufactured since the 1970s, they are still not widely available. Nevertheless, PCL is found in widely differing guises. It is sold in pellet form (more or less as delivered by the manufacturer) and in brightly-coloured rods, as a 'fun' material.

ABOVE: *Making a wicker-like donkey's head in polycaprolactone over a clay original.*

Clear cast polyester ball; one of many cast in plaster waste moulds and polished up.

Clear Casting

If you want to make optically-clear castings to imitate glass or crystal objects, there are water-clear versions of the three main casting resins. Each has it own properties.

* Clear polyester resin is the cheapest and most widely available. It is the weakest of the three (thin-walled objects smash if dropped), but this also makes it the easiest to sand and polish to a glass-like finish. Some products have the same refractive index as glass and can be reinforced with open-weave glass cloth with a minimal effect on transparency. Polyester also has the highest shrinkage, which may lead to problems with distortion and surface defects. Like all polyesters, it contains styrene monomer, the vapour of which is hazardous.
* Clear urethane is very much tougher than polyester and has negligible shrinkage, but costs three or four times as much. Being so much tougher, it is more difficult to polish. Resin–hardener ratios (although often a convenient 1:1) are fixed, so different products must be used for small, delicate castings

and large bulky ones to avoid undercuring or overheating. The main disadvantage, however, is that the hardener contains diisocyanate compounds, which are toxic even in minute quantities.

✳ Clear epoxies are less widely available; they are similar to urethane in price and working properties. Skin contact, in particular with the hardener, can result in burns, absorption of toxins and dermatitis.

Colourants can be bought for all three types of resin; they can be tinted with spirit-soluble dyes or just with dry pigments. All the resins are low-viscosity mixes, minimizing the risk of trapped air bubbles (although vacuum treatment is necessary to remove them completely), but with the consequence that they can be cast only into moulds suitable for self-levelling liquids. This may make the moulds for thin-walled or hollow objects more complex.

Moulds are usually made from silicone or urethane rubber for multiple casts, or to retain the polished surface of an original. Plaster waste moulds can be used for one-off jobs where it is practicable to sand and polish the cast.

It is possible to use a 'lost wax' approach with plaster moulds. An object is modelled or turned in wax, on a core of plaster-clad polystyrene if it is hollow. A plaster mould is then built up around it and the wax is melted out by baking or boiling. The mould is flooded with release agent and left to dry, and then filled with resin. When the resin has cured, the mould is broken away from the cast.

Clear polyester usually cures with a tacky surface where it has been exposed to air or moisture. This may eventually dry out but can be removed with neat washing-up liquid. There may also be problems with the polyester releasing from silicone moulds: incompletely cured silicone produces surface tackiness on the cast and a crazed texture as the cast cures and shrinks. Post-cure silicone moulds by baking

---

Breakaway Items

Breakable cast items – china ornaments, for instance – involve a particular problem: how to achieve a convincing 'smash' without shards flying into the eyes of performers and the front-row audience.

The solution almost always involves a compromise over the noise produced or where the action takes place. When the danger of flying debris is extreme or the mess needs to be cleared quickly, it is common practice to paint a layer of latex or latex-based glue on the object, although the resulting smash looks and sounds disappointing. With or without the latex layer, probably the best material for mimicking ceramic objects is plaster – if it is allowed to dry out fully, the breaking noise is quite convincing. It is cheap and demoulds quickly. Nearly all shapes need to be hollow; plaster can be poured into rubber moulds and rotated, painted into more open moulds or thickened with colloidal silica and pressed in. The aim with any plaster breakaway effect should be to get the debris swept up before it is walked on, since the plaster is reduced to dust. Polymer plasters break convincingly and do less damage to floors if walked on. There are also proprietary resins and waxes produced specifically for breakaway effects. The emphasis with these tends to be on a convincing smash, rather than on safety.

---

them in a low oven after their initial room-temperature cure.

White Metals

These are alloys of bright silver appearance and low melting point, used for making costume jewellery and other small metal objects. There is a variety of alloys on the market, differing in price, ease of polishing, ability to cast

White metal casting. The original prepared for moulding.

BELOW LEFT: Pouring the first part of the silicone mould.

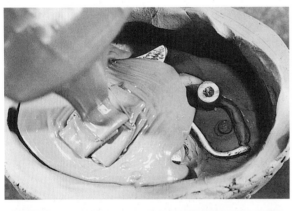

ABOVE: Pouring molten alloy into the mould, embedded in sand in case of leakage.

LEFT: The finished cast, with pouring gate still attached.

thin or delicate parts and so on. Although the majority contain lead, most suppliers also offer lead-free alloys, which are much safer to use.

Very small quantities of metal may be melted in a ladle held in a blowtorch flame, and larger amounts in a small, heavy saucepan on a gas or electric ring. The optimum temperature for pouring moulds is considerably higher than the melting point: an alloy that melts at 240°C pours at around 300°C. This can be measured accurately with a suitable thermometer or judged by experience from the behaviour of a piece of wood dipped in the molten metal. The dross that forms on the surface of the melt must be skimmed back before pouring it to stop it from entering the mould; use a spoon or a piece of bent steel wire.

White metals are usually cast into moulds made from high-temperature silicone rubber (not all silicones are suitable; check with the supplier or manufacturer). Jewellery manufacturers use rotational casting machines that fill multiple moulds by centrifugal force. The occasional user is more likely to use gravity to pour individual moulds by hand. Except in the case of complex shapes, two-part moulds are used; an ingate for the metal and vents for the escape of air are cut into the face of one part of the mould. These should be arranged so that the molten metal passes down the ingate and along a runner to enter the mould at the lowest point so that it fills it from the bottom up; the vents are placed at the top at places where air would otherwise be trapped. Pouring continues until metal appears at the top of the vents.

Dusting the mould with talc or graphite powder helps both the flow of metal and the escape of air. Warming the moulds may also be necessary to get the metal to flow into fine detail. Do this either by heating the mould in an oven or by pouring one or two preparatory casts; these can always be remelted.

Rougher casts can be taken from plaster moulds, again dusted with graphite or talc. Make sure the mould has completely dried out and that the parts still fit together well. If in doubt, bury the mould in sand before pouring. For one-off casts of complex shapes, lost-wax casting is possible – add a wax rod to the original to form the ingate and runner, pieces of wire for the vents and a wax plug to make a drain for the molten wax at the bottom of the system. Encase in a proprietary investment compound or plaster made up with thin clay wash instead of water (it must be strong enough to withstand the casting process, but weak enough to chip away later). When set, pull out the wires to form the vents and bake the mould in a very hot oven until all trace of wax has disappeared. Leave to cool. Plug the drain with fresh plaster and leave this to dry out. Before pouring the mould, heat again to near the melting point of the metal.

All white-metal castings shrink considerably as they cool. If necessary, allow for this by making the originals larger. A larger body of metal in the ingate and runner helps to minimize the effect of shrinkage and prevent the castings from distorting as they shrink.

White Metal Health and Safety

- Always melt metal in a properly ventilated area – if the alloy contains lead use local exhaust ventilation or a suitable respirator.
- Wear goggles and leather gloves when melting and when handling molten metal.
- Make sure that no moisture can enter molten metal and that the moulds are completely dry before pouring; tiny quantities of water turning to steam may spray molten metal over a wide area.
- Castings, an excess of metal and melting vessels remain hot for a long time. Never use water to speed cooling.
- If you must use a lead alloy, wear gloves when handling, filing or polishing.

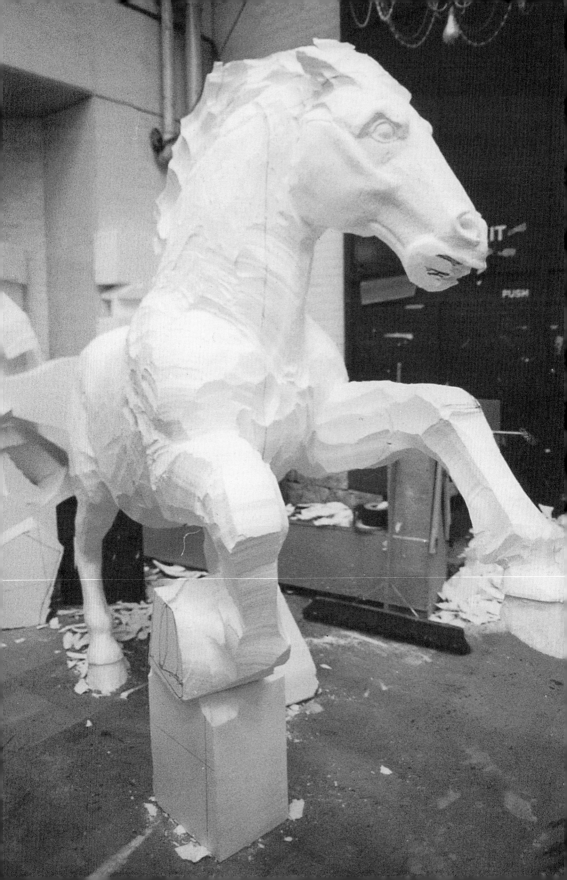

7 WORKING WITH EXPANDED POLYSTYRENE

Lightweight and easily worked, expanded polystyrene allows complex three-dimensional shapes to be produced directly by carving, thus avoiding lengthy casting processes and allowing large forms to be kept to reasonable weights. The price to be paid for its light weight and ease of cutting is that expanded polystyrene is inconveniently weak for stage use, usually requiring some kind of protective coating to be applied after shaping. Coatings can also be used to modify the surface texture of the work and to improve its fire resistance. A related material, extruded polystyrene, is denser, stronger and very much finer in texture, and thus can be worked in more detail, but it still requires protection and fire-retardant treatment.

AVAILABILITY

Expanded polystyrene is manufactured for packaging and for the construction industry, which uses it for insulation and for concrete shuttering, in 2,440mm × 1,220mm × 610mm (8ft × 4ft × 2ft) blocks (though bigger pieces are sometimes available). The supplier slices these to order into smaller thicknesses, according to your specification. They may also offer more elaborate cutting services such as the production of cylinders and spheres. Suppliers cut polystyrene with hot wires (*see* below), giving clean, straight cuts, though sheets are often bowed.

Expanded polystyrene is available in a range of densities. 'Standard' is defined as 12 to 15oz/cu ft (which, strangely, is the same as 12 to 15kg/cu m); this is adequate for most stage use, although heavy or extra heavy density (EHD) at 18 or 24oz (or kg) is stronger and will take finer detail; these are particularly useful where thin sections are involved. Lower than normal densities, while cheaper, are considered too fragile for most carving work but might still be usable, depending on the nature of the work. Polystyrene is available with a fire-retardant additive (FRA), for perhaps 10 per cent over the basic cost and should always be specified for prop making use – and even if it is never going to appear on stage, you do not want untreated material hanging around the workshop.

Often known by one manufacturer's trade name, Styrofoam, extruded polystyrene is used almost exclusively for insulation and is available in a much smaller range of sizes: sheets are generally 8ft × 2ft (2,440mm × 610mm), in thicknesses up to 5in (125mm). It is three to four times the price of expanded polystyrene and is usually pale blue, pink or green in colour, depending on the brand. Densities, surface

LEFT: A horse, rather larger than life-size, being carved from expanded polystyrene. Parts of the head are finished, but the rest still shows signs of rough cutting with a hot wire.

Scrim drying on a small carved panel.

BELOW: *Polystyrene carving tools – a sharpening steel, various knives and a wire brush.*

finish and fire-retardancy vary between different manufacturers and grades; suppliers can help you to select what you need.

CUTTING AND SHAPING

As it is so soft, polystyrene can be cut and shaped easily with many kinds of tool, all with their own uses and characteristics:

* Handsaws are a fast but messy way to cut blocks or rough shapes. Use a well-set panel saw for straight cuts and an old-fashioned bow saw for curves. Cutting square takes practice.
* Band saws rapidly convert 8ft × 4ft sheets to smaller sizes and rough out basic shapes before carving. They cut quickly, cleanly and square and can handle intricate curves. They need to be large – say a 600mm throat – for all but the smallest work.
* A bench saw (circular saw) makes straight cuts in thinner sheets, although the thicker blade produces far more dust than a bandsaw.
* An electric jigsaw is useful for cutting and shaping, particularly when extra-long blades can be found. It really doesn't matter much what type of blade you use.
* Knives of all kinds are useful (as long as they are sharp). What you use is a matter of personal preference; experiment with different

Polystyrene textures. Left to right: knife-cut, wire-brushed, hot-wired and bandsawn. The top half of each sample has been 'wafted' with a hot-air gun.

BELOW: *A hot-air gun has been used extensively in these two carvings to create masonry textures.*

types. A plain, narrow-bladed kitchen knife 150 to 200mm long is a useful carving tool, while a similar but wider blade can be used to remove bulk quickly by stabbing and twisting the foam away in lumps. Long, thin, flexible knives cut curves and concave surfaces.

* A wire brush provides a fast (but messy) way to remove material when carving, which many people find preferable to the use of a knife. It allows for the vigorous sketching of flowing lines, and the inability to create detail encourages a concentration on basic forms.
* Coarse sandpaper can be used in the same way at smaller scales, while finer grades may be used to smooth out surfaces or refine curves. When smoothing, minimize break-out by keeping the sandpaper clear of loose beads and using gentle pressure.
* Electric disc or belt sanders achieve results quickly, although dust extraction at source becomes essential and the heat generated at the surface of the polystyrene may become a problem. Hand-held electric routers may be used in more or less the same way as they are on wood, leaving a clean, crisp surface. Again, a lot of airborne dust is produced if it is not extracted at source.

127

✳ A hot-air gun of the kind sold for stripping paint can be wafted over a carved surface to level out tool marks, melt away fine dust left by sanding and form a tough crust on the work. It can also be used as a texturing tool in itself, for instance, in the carving of masonry – but only as much as to produce a slight shrinking of the polystyrene, since more vigorous melting may produce unacceptable levels of styrene vapour.

TURNING POLYSTYRENE

Last but not least among shaping tools is the lathe. Turning polystyrene is fast; it can produce hollow forms of some sophistication and

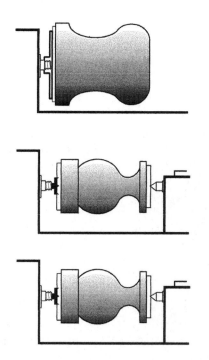

Ways of holding polystyrene in the lathe: on a faceplate (using contact glue), between centres (using sandpaper-covered ply discs and tailstock pressure) and a mandrel.

extremely large turnings. Surface coatings (*see* below) can be applied, sanded or themselves turned while the work is still in the lathe.

The fact that the work tends to be large means that lathes designed for woodturning are often simply not big enough, and the speeds available may be too high for the large diameters involved. As a result, a lot of work takes place on custom-built lathes, simply constructed owing to the low weight of the polystyrene and the slow running speeds required. But a wood lathe with a suitable bottom speed – 500 or 600rpm at the most – is still useful, especially if it allows outboard work on a faceplate.

There are two basic processes in polystyrene turning. In the first, which mimics traditional woodturning, the lathe is powered by a geared-down electric motor (or an energetic assistant) and the cut is made by placing a sharp tool, backed by a solid tool-rest, in the way of the rotating polystyrene. In the second, the cutting is done with a fixed, powered tool (such as a router or hot-wire) and the work is rotated slowly past the tool by hand. This latter process is much slower and more 'technical', but has advantages in that an unpowered lathe is much simpler to make, and for the production turning of many identical pieces.

When turning outboard, there is little option but to glue the polystyrene to a ply-wood disc attached to the faceplate. Between centres, there is more choice. The stock may again be glued to a faceplate, and the tailstock centre used simply for support. A ply disc can be glued to each end of the stock, one to be driven by a spur while the other turns on the tailstock centre. A quick way to mount small work is to make two discs, one indented for the drive spur and the other punched for the tailstock centre, and to glue coarse sandpaper to them. Lumps of polystyrene can then be mounted in the lathe using pressure from the tailstock quill, the sandpaper providing a friction grip.

TOP: *Large turning – this picture gives some idea of the mess that turning polystyrene creates.*

ABOVE: *Large turnings being scrimmed.*

Often, a polystyrene turning needs to be bored out down its centre so that it can slide over a structural element such as a steel tube. The arrangement illustrated at the bottom of page 28 is quick to make (and works for wooden turnings too). The central hole is bored first and a piece of the tube just slightly longer than the turning stock placed in it. The ends of the tube are caught in the holes in the discs, ensuring that it is central, while the polystyrene is driven by glue or sandpaper on the discs as before.

Any polystyrene turning is an extremely messy process, and the logistics of dealing with the waste created should not be underestimated – clearing up can take longer than the work itself.

HOT WIRES

These use an electric current to heat a resistance wire to a temperature at which it will melt through the polystyrene. There is hot wire equipment on the market: the fact that many people still make their own is due to economy and the apparent simplicity of the task. The wire may be of steel, but relatively high currents or voltages may be required – alloys optimized for use as heating elements such as nickel chrome (Nichrome) are more efficient and last longer. They are more expensive and harder to find; polystyrene suppliers, who use a great deal of it, will sometimes donate a few offcuts, which may be all you need. Thicknesses between 24 and 20SWG (0.4 and 0.8mm) are the best for general use. The electricity supply should be at a low voltage for safety's sake – either a motorbike or car battery at 6 or 12V, or a transformer offering a range of voltages in that region and capable of supplying up to 10A. The gauge (thickness) of the wire determines the resistance per unit length, and the wattage per unit length required to raise the wire to the operating temperature. So if you are using a battery and therefore a fixed voltage, you will need to find the right length of wire for that voltage. The important thing is to use the lowest

Sanding a column capital on the lathe.

wire temperature that will still cut, to minimize the production of harmful gases; the wire must never be allowed to glow. Wires may be connected between two handles and used freehand for carving large blocks (in which case care must be taken not to 'loop' the wire, shortening it and possibly overloading the power supply), or stretched in some permanent position and the polystyrene manoeuvred through it (where the means used to tension the wire must allow for the fact that the wire gets longer as it heats up). Thicker wire (2 to 4mm) can be bent to the profile of a moulding; this kind of work requires much higher wattages and some skill in bending

OPPOSITE PAGE:

TOP: A hot-wire cutter in use – the wire is the profiled shape on the left.

BOTTOM: Close-up of the profiled wire in the preceding photograph. The other electrical contact is beneath the table.

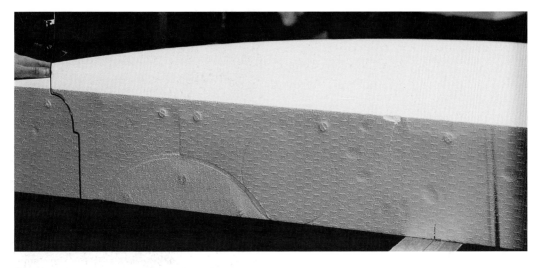

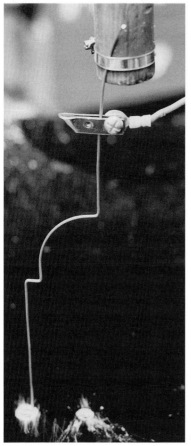

Hot Wire Health and Safety

Melting polystyrene releases styrene vapour, which is harmful by inhalation. Intermittent use of a properly set up hot wire in a well-ventilated workshop is unlikely to produce levels exceeding Occupational Exposure Limits, but exposure should nevertheless be kept to a minimum. Always take the following precautions:

- Use the lowest wire temperature possible. Only where there is a need for the cut to be made quickly should a hotter wire be used. If possible use equipment that offers fine control of voltage; otherwise, increase wire length to reduce temperature.
- As the wire breaks through at the end of a cut, its temperature rises quickly, and small pieces of polystyrene adhering to it are burnt off. If possible, turn off the power as soon as the cut is finished and remove these small pieces mechanically before turning back on.
- Always work in a well-ventilated area. If possible, use local exhaust ventilation to extract fumes from close to the source; otherwise, use a fan to blow them away.
- If necessary, wear a respirator fitted with a filter for particulates and organic vapour. Using a respirator is a last resort, not a substitute for proper ventilation.
- Be aware of the dangers of burns and electric shock. Wearing standard rigger gloves protects against both.

the wire to avoid producing cold spots that impede the progress of the cut. Wires of this thickness require a higher wattage, and therefore a larger and more expensive transformer, to reach cutting temperature than do thin stretched wires.

JOINING POLYSTYRENE

Fixing polystyrene to itself or to other materials is best done with contact adhesives designed for the purpose, since many contact glues contain solvents that will attack and dissolve polystyrene. Get advice from your supplier, or look for glues where the mastic is dissolved in hexane rather than toluene. These adhesives require a close fit between the parts to be joined; a thin, even layer is spread on each surface, the solvent is allowed to evaporate (5 to 10min) and the two parts are brought together. The bond is immediate, allowing for no repositioning. Keep glue layers as thin as possible when carving or hot-wire cutting is to be carried out through the glue line. Cheaper glues on offer from insulation firms tend to have a much thicker consistency, and a join made with them can stop a hot wire or a knife.

Latex-based glues can be used as contact adhesives in the same way, although they are much slower drying and present even worse problems for hot wires and carving knives. Epoxy resins offer bonds of extremely high strength, although they are slow and inconvenient. Kept thin enough, they can be carved through, but, again, a close fit between parts is essential. The only effective gap-filling adhesive for polystyrene is rigid polyurethane foam ('expanding foam', 'brown foam'). This is available in two forms: an aerosol for filling gaps in building work (DIY shops, builders' merchants) or as two liquids to be mixed immediately before use (sold mainly for filling buoyancy compartments in boat-building and available from yacht chandlers). Both types adhere well to polystyrene and can be carved

Glues to Avoid

The product sold as 'polystyrene cement' in DIY stores is for fixing tiles to ceilings and of no use in prop work (except perhaps as a coating). That sold as 'polystyrene cement' in model shops is for gluing solid polystyrene (plastic kits, and so on) and simply makes holes in the expanded variety.

after they have cured, although they are much denser than the polystyrene around them. They give off isocyanate gases while curing and when carved, and so suitable extraction, ventilation or at least a respirator with an organic vapour filter is essential.

Spray mount and photo mount, used more or less as recommended on the can, form weak, easily broken bonds between polystyrene and itself or other materials, which may be useful for checking the assembly of work as it progresses, given the permanence of the other adhesives.

APPROACHES TO CARVING

Many people find the idea of carving daunting – much more so than modelling something out of clay, for example. The perfect white rectangle that faces them is about as different as it could be from the shape they want. They are reluctant to make the first cut in case it is wrong. But there is no need for such timidity. Like many processes, carving is a matter of finding a starting point and then proceeding in a systematic way. That first cut is unlikely to spoil things; if it does, you can always glue the piece back on or stick on a new blank piece and have another try.

In nearly all prop making situations you will have some kind of visual reference for the work; there you will find your starting point. If the prop is large, it may appear in the designer's

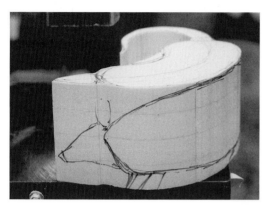

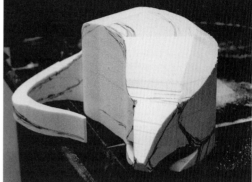

Steps in carving an armadillo in extruded polystyrene. ABOVE LEFT: *The plan view has been drawn and cut; the side view is being drawn.*

ABOVE: *After cutting the side view.*

Rounding and refining with a knife...

...and smoothing with sandpaper.

model. Such a model might be enough to work from, but usually a designer will provide more detailed images as well. These in turn may lead to further discussion – the more different types of reference there are, the more important it is to agree on why each is there. You may end with a rough model for a statue that shows the overall dimensions, separate photographs showing its pose and the style of carving, and a sketch of a detail to be added. If, however, you find yourself without enough visual information, it is important that you seek it from the designer or get hold of it yourself.

Although it is a three-dimensional job, you can approach the process of 'roughing out' a carving as a series of two-dimensional tasks. Familiarize yourself with the references and with the shape of the object you have to reproduce. Referring to the dimensions and to the object's shape, choose or cut a suitable block of polystyrene. Which view of the object – which profile – contains the most detail or information, the most 'landmarks' to help you to fill in the gaps? If this view is not among the references, you will have to draw it. Mark it out on the appropriate face of the block; if you are not working straight from the model, you may have to calculate a custom scale. Is there another view, at 90 degrees to the first, with additional detail in it? If there is, draw this next view on its own face, carefully registering it with the first drawing. Then cut out the first outline, treating it as two-dimensional, cutting square through the block with a band saw, hot wire or handsaw. Tape back the off-cuts so that you have a rectangular block once more, and cut the second outline in the same way. In most cases, cutting these first two intersecting profiles accomplishes a great deal. Cross-sections in the third plane remain rectangular, but the landmarks and basic forms established by the first two cuts enable you to progress to more free-hand carving. Occasionally, it may be worth the effort to treat the third plane in the same way: heads benefit particularly from front, side and top

views being cut like this, even though there are many more offcuts to reassemble after the second cut than the first.

Note that the success of this process relies on being able to cut squarely through the block – this is possible with a handsaw though obviously it is much easier with a band saw or fixed hot wire.

If you are keen to cut a certain profile but the block is too big to saw that way up, consider cutting it in half down the middle and cutting the relevant profile (or perhaps two different profiles) on the two halves separately before gluing them back together. In large work where the block is made up of several sheets, a different outline can be given to each layer before gluing up.

A different way to arrive at a 'rough' for carving uses the same principle of cutting two-dimensional outlines, but instead of starting out with a single block from which material is then removed, involves cutting out different elements of the work separately, and combining them, kit-form, to make the rough. The best example is something like two life-sized figures entwined in dance or combat. Carving from a single block would be wasteful and time-consuming and outlines of the whole tableau too complex or hard to find to be useful. Marking and cutting a kit of heads, torsos, arms, legs and so on in appropriate positions (perhaps by drawing round helpful colleagues) from sheets of suitable thickness and then carefully assembling them allows you to experiment with the exact relationship between parts (use knitting needles or barbecue skewers to fix parts temporarily while you contemplate them), as well as being more economical.

The object of roughing out is to remove most of the waste polystyrene and swiftly arrive at the point where you can start to work with a knife or a brush. You should reach this point as familiar as possible with what it is you intend to make, and with a clear understanding of which features exist in some form in roughed-out state

Figures carved from a kit-form rough, assembled from parts made by drawing round live models.

and which are still obscured. What are the most essential differences between the rough and the reference? Locate these areas of difference – the 'biggest' things the roughing-out process could not define. Draw into the freshly cut surface with a marker pen, referring to the parts of your original mark-up that are still on the work.

In a band-sawn rough involving the intersection of two different outlines, the first task is usually to establish features that were 'overshadowed' by others and obscured during the roughing-out process. In roughs made by assembling separately formed parts, this step may not be necessary, and you will be dealing direct with the most likely shortcoming of your rough – the fact that cross-sections through it in at least one dimension are still rectangular.

The realization of rounded forms from these rectangular cross-sections is a process some beginners find difficult; they usually round off only the very corners and never quite escape from the rectangles. Luckily the answer to this is simply to be bolder with the first few cuts that you take from each corner. The process of reducing a square cross-section to a circular one involves cutting the square to an octagon,

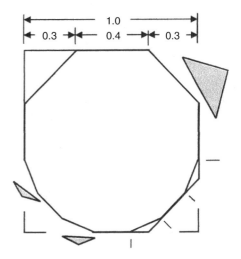

Rounding a square form. The first cuts, that take the square down to an octagon, are crucial; if the right amount is taken off, a circular section can be achieved quickly. For a true octagon, the first 45-degree cuts remove a full 30 per cent from each side of each square face. If each of the octagon's sides is then cut in the same way to produce a sixteen-sided section, the rest can be done with sandpaper.

135

Polystyrene Health and Safety

- Dust is created in large quantities when sanding, turning, routing or using power saws. Avoid inhaling it. Use extraction equipment when possible (it protects other people sharing or passing through your workspace) and wear a disposable P2 mask. Polystyrene dust is very light – it becomes airborne easily and takes a long time to settle. Static electricity can cause it to cling to clothes and surfaces. Use a vacuum cleaner regularly.
- Organic vapours are released by the solvents used in contact adhesives. Always work in a well-ventilated area and when large areas of glue are needed use LEV or at least a respirator with an organic vapour filter. Styrene vapour is released in small quantities whenever polystyrene is cut, and in larger

quantities by hot wires and hot-air guns. Work in a well-ventilated area and use local exhaust ventilation on large pieces of work. Never let a hot wire get above black heat. A glowing wire releases toxic gases. Use hot-air guns only for subtle changes to surface texture, and always keep the gun moving.
- Carving knives can inflict serious injury. Always cut away from your body and your other hand. Keep other knives in a box or tray, not loose on the work surface. Do not rush, and do not use sharp knives when your concentration is impaired by illness or tiredness, or when you are likely to be distracted by other people.
- Epoxy resins and band saws present a number of hazards: *see* the health and safety advice relating to their use.

the octagon to a sixteen-sided shape, and so on. Draw a square and a circle that just fits within it. Draw across the corners of the square to make an octagon, then again across the octagon's corners to give sixteen sides. You can see from this drawing how much the first cut on each corner must remove and that, by the time you have made the second cuts, your form is well on the way to being cylindrical.

Although a cylinder is good practice, you are more likely to be carving a leg or a tree, where the shape of the cross-section changes continuously. You need to work out key cross-sections and how they change from one to the next, before you can go on. Trying ideas out on a piece of scrap polystyrene or a lump of modelling clay may help, as will drawing on paper or direct on to the polystyrene.

Try to use the knife or brush as if drawing with it. Keep studying the references and considering the work as a series of two-dimensional cuts. Look at it from different angles and from a distance; get someone else, with a fresh eye, to give constructive criticism. If possible, use scaled measurements for accuracy. Most carving of sculpture involves carefully scaling up from a clay or wax model, not spontaneously chiselling away.

To sum up: successful carving comes from good references and a suitable roughing-out strategy. Accuracy in drawing and cutting the initial outlines will save time and greatly simplify the subsequent carving.

COATINGS FOR POLYSTYRENE AND STYROFOAM

Both expanded and extruded polystyrene need to be coated to protect them from the rigours of stage use. There is a wide choice of coatings; which you choose will depend on your budget and on what you want from the coating. Some offer little more than some protection and a 'paint-friendly' surface, while others provide fire resistance, great strength or the possibility of over-modelling details.

The options fall into these main groups:

* scrimming and papering: gluing on a layer of fabric or paper to form a skin;
* off-the-shelf products offering fire protection, strength and the possibility of texturing or sanding smooth;
* plaster-based mixtures;
* glass-reinforced plastic.

SCRIMMING

This common treatment is often applied before other coatings or as a base for painting. As a technique, scrimming is much older than the use of polystyrene; it has long been used to hold together different parts of a construction and to give them a common texture on which to paint. It involves sticking a lightweight cotton fabric such as butter muslin to the surface of the polystyrene with glue, typically size (animal glue) or PVA.

Size has a slippery quality when wet, which makes scrimming with it faster than with the much stickier PVA. The low viscosity of size when hot means that it goes on very thinly, allowing fine detail to show through. As it cools,

Scrimming.

Making Size

1. Measure the required amount of water into a plastic or metal bucket.
2. Add size or pearl glue at the rate of 125g/ltr of water. Stir well.
3. Then, either place in a water bath at 85°C or in a larger metal bucket containing a few inches of water and heat gently on a gas or electric ring. Try to keep the water just below its boiling point – overheated size loses its adhesive power.
4. Stir regularly until all the glue has dissolved. If you want to add powder pigment to give the work a base colour, pour a little size off into another container, mix the pigment into it and return it to the pot.
5. Reheat it if it thickens or gels. Do not reheat size more than 24hr old. Throw unwanted size away before it rots.

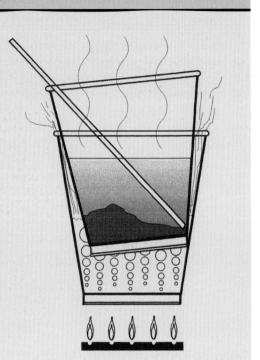

Cooking up size in two buckets. Never let the outer one boil dry!

it thickens and the scrim layer becomes more substantial. It is never more than a delicate skin, but it protects work from minor damage, makes a good surface for painting and adds very little weight. Scrimming with PVA is slower, but the result is somewhat tougher.

To apply the scrim, cut muslin into pieces of a suitable size for the work. Paint a layer of glue on first before dropping the muslin into it and working it in with a wet brush. When covering complex three-dimensional surfaces, work outwards from the middle of each piece to allow fabric to go down into all the detail. Finish working in each piece before applying the next. Big overlaps between pieces are not necessary. A little pigment added to the size will help you to spot gaps.

There are many possible variations on the basic scrimming process. Other fabrics may be used, or various kinds of paper: brown wrapping paper scrumpled tightly and opened out again repeatedly develops a leathery quality, for example. Scrimming may also be used to reinforce constructions where polystyrene has been used with other materials and to unify the different materials visually.

After scrimming, size can be mixed with an inert filler such as whiting, marble dust or talc to make a creamy liquid similar to old-fashioned gesso. Brushed on in multiple layers, it can be sanded to a smooth, silky finish when dry. It is best to dilute the size with about half as much water again; this makes the sanding easier and thick coats are less prone to cracking.

Polystyrene sink, scrimmed, painted with a crude gesso of size and whiting, and glazed. With practical taps.

The finished product is quite delicate, but can be strengthened with a final coat of neat size or glazed with epoxy resin or an acrylic varnish. Careful sanding and varnishing can produce a finish comparable to glazed porcelain. Again, pigments may be used to tint the mixture; for a brilliant white use titanium dioxide.

Avoid inhaling or ingesting the dust produced by sanding any of these mixtures – size dust alone is very unpleasant in the mouth and most fillers contain silicates. Always wear a dust mask, and clean up regularly.

PROPRIETARY COATINGS

A number of branded products are used as coatings for polystyrene in theatre work. Most are water-based emulsions of synthetic polymers with added fillers, and are brushed, sprayed or trowelled on. Rosco's 'Foamcoat' is a heavily filled acrylic mixture aimed specifically at the prop-making market. It dries to an extremely tough, fire-retardant finish that can be sanded to a fine finish, but it is hard work: inevitably there is a trade-off between ease of sanding and the toughness of the film. Evode

'Idenden Brushcote' is an industrial insulation product that dries to a flexible plastic film. It can be heavily textured or made smoother by the use of a wet brush or rag when partially dry. LPL's 'Firecheck' is an excellent fire-retardant coating; it can be smoothed in the same way as 'Idenden', or used as a quick coating for unseen surfaces. There are probably many other similar products available to be adopted from other industries. Once it is found that a product serves its needs, the theatre tends to stick with it. There is usually a reason for the popularity of such materials, but it is also worth experimenting with what other firms have to offer.

PLASTER-BASED COATINGS

These have several advantages over air-drying coatings. Plaster hardens as a result of a chemical reaction, not evaporation, and its setting time is not affected by thickness, making it possible to model detail over the polystyrene. Its usually fast setting time can be reliably retarded for optimum working time. Lastly, reinforcements and other additives may be varied to suit the job. Although

139

it is possible to use plaster without reinforcement, it must be quite thick if it is not to be delicate; usually some kind of fibrous reinforcement is added to make a stronger composite material. Neat plaster is also one of life's most unrewarding modelling materials and needs a thickener and/or a finely chopped reinforcement to make it more responsive.

The use of polymer solutions in place of water (*see* the section on plaster-based materials on page 116) produces tougher coatings; as well as the plaster itself being stronger, it adheres better to the reinforcement.

Reinforcements for plaster include jute scrim, as used in plaster mould-making, and glass fibre in the form of open-weave cloth or multiaxial woven rovings. To cover large areas with these materials, a layer of wet plaster is applied first and the reinforcement bedded into it; for local strengthening, strips may be dipped in plaster and then applied. For heavy texturing or over-modelling, chopped reinforcement that can be mixed direct with the plaster is of more use – dry paper pulp (cellulose fibre) or cotton microfibres (sold as an additive for epoxy resin) are particularly good.

ABOVE: **Bark texture made with a polymer plaster/sawdust mixture.**

Armadillo, before painting, coated with polymer plaster, dusted with talc and impressed with texture.

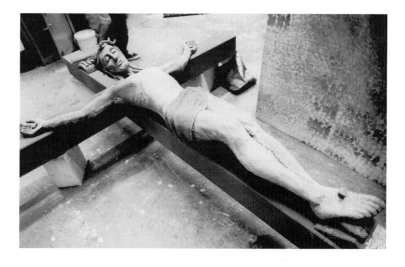

Crucifix (see p.6) coated by spraying coloured polymer plaster with a hopper gun, and smoothing selectively with a wet brush as it set.

The most reliable retardant for plaster is trisodium citrate. This can be bought in solution, or more economically as a powder that you dissolve yourself. A useful working dilution is 100g of powder per litre of water. Add the solution to the mixing water with a teaspoon or syringe before adding the plaster; how much you need will depend on the plaster you are using. As a very rough guide, 10ml (2 teaspoons) per litre of mixing water will double the setting time.

Thickeners include colloidal or fumed silica, sold for thickening polyester and epoxy resins, that turn plaster into a smooth modelling dough. Fine sawdust and/or polystyrene dust (look in dust extractor bags) make a good texturing paste. Dry paper pulp thickens as well as reinforcing.

Finally, one of the simplest plaster-based coatings is plaster bandage, with a splash of Polyvinyl Acetate or an acrylic medium added to the water to retard and strengthen it. It is quick to apply and preserves much of the underlying detail; it can be worked into a smooth finish, or it can be used to add modelled detail.

GRP COATINGS

Epoxy resin can be used with glass-fibre reinforcement to create coatings of very high strength; when it is cured, the polystyrene can be cut away to leave, a tough, hollow shell. Epoxy forms powerful bonds to other materials or hardware items and can be mixed with fillers such as colloidal silica, talc or marble dust to a consistency that can be modelled over the basic glass laminate. The epoxy/silica combination can be applied to work on the lathe and turned as it cures. Epoxy resin and its hardeners present considerable health hazards. Always avoid all skin contact.

Polyester resin is a standard material for the production of glass-fibre laminates; it contains styrene monomer. This solvent dissolves both expanded and extruded polystyrene on contact; its vapour is harmful and must be extracted from the work area. Nevertheless, many prop makers prefer it to epoxy – it is about a quarter of the price, faster and easier to use, and is compatible with a wider range of glass reinforcement. Its use requires that the polystyrene is completely sealed, either by several coats of paint or by a layer of aluminium foil.

141

8   UPHOLSTERY

An upholstery job may be as simple as re-covering a drop-in seat for a dining chair, or as complex as completely upholstering an elaborate sofa.

Stage upholstery differs from the 'real' thing in that physical comfort is less of a priority. In fact, it may be undesirable – it is common to insert plywood under the cushions of sofas and armchairs so that actors can get up from them more easily. It is also not often required to last as long. The main practical effect of this shift of emphasis is that, although the cover fabrics may be the same, what lies beneath is likely to be much simpler, with plywood used instead of webbing or springing and foam as the main filling, unless it is felt that more elaborate techniques will contribute significantly to the look of the work.

An upholstered window seat.

Basics

Most upholstery includes three components: support, filling and cover. Within each there are many possible variations.

Support

This is the load-bearing bottom layer; in traditional upholstery it is commonly made of jute webbing stretched each way across the work and covered with a piece of hessian. In more modern upholstery it might be made of rubber webbing or steel tension springs. Stage upholstery is much more likely to be supported on thin plywood, for speed of construction and firmness and because it provides a surface to which foam can be glued to create the desired shape. At close quarters or when the underside of the upholstery will be seen, fine jute scrim or black casement can be dressed over the ply.

Fillings

These are what give the upholstery its shape and depth. Traditional fillings are made of various animal and vegetable fibres and are usually applied in two layers. The first is of dense, coarse fibre tied to the supporting hessian, covered with scrim and stitched to form the shape of the work; the second is a softer layer, typically of cotton felt, laid over the top to fair the shape and provide comfort. Sprung work would have hourglass compression springs between the webbing and the first stuffing. Modern upholstery, both of contemporary designs and reproduction work, uses polyurethane foam as the main filling. Nearly all stage prop upholstery follows this lead, and the shaping and covering of foam forms the major part of it. Often the foam is wrapped in a layer of polyester wadding to soften the shape and prevent the foam from 'catching' the cover fabric.

Cover

This is the topmost, visible layer of the upholstery, traditionally a hardwearing textile or real or imitation leather. On stage, where durability is not as important as appearance, less substantial (and cheaper) fabrics are often used. Here, a lining of calico or similar material is best used beneath top covers. The covering stage may also include applying buttoning and trims such as gimp, piping or braid, which are used to decorate edges and to hide the staples holding the cover on.

Working with Foam

Several types of foam are used for upholstery, all sometimes referred to as 'foam rubber' because the first one, historically, was foam latex. This is still used at the top end of the market,

ABOVE: Several upholstery trims. From left: looped ruche, rope trim, three types of gimp, two sizes of cord, nail head strip and two 'novelty' trims.

Foams. From the top down: plastazote, chipfoam and two grades of urethane upholstery foam.

but is unlikely to end up on stage because of its price. Most of the kind of custom upholstery into which props work falls is done with polyurethane foam in one of two forms: as new foam, or as the denser chipfoam or 'recon', in which offcuts of new foam have been shredded and bonded into blocks under pressure. Both come in sheets of around 2m × 1.5m in a range of standard thicknesses, or can be cut to size by the supplier to suit your needs.

New foam varies both in density (the amount of plastic in it per unit volume, which determines how durable it is) and hardness (the force it takes to squash it, determining the kind of comfort it offers). Denser foams are more expensive, particularly in softer grades. The two measures are expressed numerically, the density in kg/cu m and the hardness in newtons. Typical densities range from 24 (light) up to 50 (heavy), and hardnesses from 50 (very soft) to 230 (very firm). Thus a foam described as 33/180 is a medium-weight, firm product probably intended for seating, while 24/080 is lightweight and soft and more suited to backs; 50/135 is very dense but still quite soft, and therefore a top-quality seat foam.

Chipfoam is usually described by density alone, still expressed (perversely) in pounds per cubic foot. Most suppliers carry only two, 5 and 8lb – around 80 and 130 kg/cu m, and therefore much denser than new foam. They are correspondingly harder – 8lb is the kind of material gymnasium mats are made of – and are used for arms, stiffened edges and so on.

CUTTING

The tool of choice is the Bosch 1575 electric foam cutter, which uses two reciprocating blades to cut foam up to 300mm thick. However, the price of these means that a workshop doing only occasional bits of upholstery will probably make do with something less effective.

The next best device is a band saw fitted with a straight knife band. It is a fast way to dimension blocks and to cut bevels, circles and profiles. Some kind of extension table will be needed around the machine for cutting into whole sheets. An ordinary saw blade of about six or more teeth per inch also works quite well, except on light trimming cuts; if there is very little foam on one side of the blade it can get dragged down into the throat plate. Straight knife blades are available for jigsaws, and work well on thinner foam. There needs to be firm support without interfering with the blade.

Cutting foam with a knife blade in the bandsaw.

Electric carving knives work if you have patience and can keep the blades very sharp – not easy with scalloped cutting edges. They are lighter than jigsaws and have a longer cutting edge. The wand-like relationship between hand and blade makes things like bevels easier.

Lastly, a plain kitchen carving knife 9 or 10in long is a very useful tool, at a fraction of the price of any of the above. The trick is to keep it razor-sharp, either with a traditional 'steel' or a disc-type sharpener.

JOINING

The best way to stick foam to itself or to other materials is with a contact adhesive, available either in tins, to be spread on to the foam, or in aerosol cans. When spread on, the thixotropic types go on most easily and tidily. Spray glues are much faster, but more expensive. In either case, the glue is applied to both surfaces and left to dry for a few minutes; the two parts are then brought together and the bond is more or less instant; no repositioning is possible.

Most aerosols produce a fairly controllable spray in a narrow fan. A nozzle insert can be turned through 90 degrees to orient the spray, and low, medium or high output selected by moving the nozzle itself. Keep the nozzle clean by inverting the can and spraying through after each use, or it will soon produce only a single jet of glue. Although most contact glues on the market are solvent-based, water-based products that can compete in performance are now beginning to emerge (for instance, 3M 'Fastbond 100', available in spray cans as well as bulk tins). Glue on a strip of calico or other fabric to reinforce joins under tension. Where the join is to wood, it can also be stapled.

SHAPING FOAM

The profiles of the upholstery are as important to the accuracy of a piece of period furniture as the woodwork, and to achieve these forms in foam is one of the basic tasks. The flatness of a slab of new foam is not a shape that features in traditional upholstery and may look very clumsy. Even if you have not got a specific reference for accurate reproduction, try to make surfaces in danger of coming out flat slightly crowned, or concave to simulate upholstery that has collapsed with age.

The lively shapes of period work are best achieved by building foam up in layers, rather than by 'sculpting' a single block. A small piece of foam placed under the middle of a seat will give it fullness and avoid a flat zone in the middle; surround or support a seat with a strip of firmer foam to create a 'feather edge'. The scroll end of a chaise longue is easiest to form in thin layers. The topmost layer should always be a continuous sheet, with blocks used to provide bulk placed underneath.

Rolled edges can be formed by cutting the foam oversize and chamfering it, gluing it to the support with the chamfered side down. The angle of the chamfer determines the profile of the roll. With steep chamfers, and with harder foams, the tension involved may be considerable, and it is worth reinforcing the glue join with a strip of fabric or by pulling the whole piece down in calico (*see* the section on calico,

---

Foam-Cutting Tools

Basic Tools
- tape measure and straightedge
- marker pens for foam, chalk for fabrics
- long, plain kitchen knife (and a way of sharpening it) or electric carving knife
- large shears for cutting fabric and small sewing scissors
- pin hammer for tacks or hand staple gun
- hot glue gun
- dressmaker's pins
- straight and curved needles for hand sewing
- upholsterer's skewers – 100mm long wire pins, one end sharpened and the other formed into an eye, used to fix fabric temporarily to woodwork
- sewing machine

Advanced Tools
- electric foam cutter or band saw with knife blade
- pneumatic or electric staple gun

Building up foam structures for upholstery. Top, a plain drop-in seat; bevelled edges are pulled down with calico to create a rolled edge. Beneath it, the same seat with a 'crown' produced by inserting a small piece of dense foam in the middle. Beneath this, a cushion made by gluing together two bevelled pieces of foam. Bottom, the shaped scroll end of a chaise formed in layers.

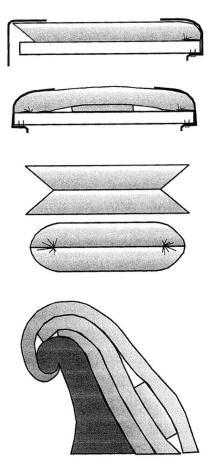

below). Round nosings are most easily made by taking foam half the required thickness and folding it double. Whatever the process, accurate measuring, marking and cutting are necessary for consistent and predictable results.

POLYESTER

Although it is also available as loose fibre for filling cushions, polyester is most often used in the form of wadding. It softens the look and feel of foam and provides a top layer with plenty of give for fluting or deep buttoning. Various thicknesses are available, from 2oz/sq yd (70g/sq m), a light cover for a foam seat or cushion, to 14oz (475g), which can take deep buttoning or be rolled or folded to fill a lightweight cushion without any foam. The way in which the polyester fibres have been bonded also affects the feel, with surface-, centre- and through-bonded waddings being progressively firmer. When it is laid over foam, a very light spray of glue will hold it in place; often even this is not needed. When using it to wrap foam for cushions, join edges by gluing or stitching.

CALICO

This is another basic material with a number of uses. The most important is as a lining, separating cover fabric from filling, where it is used to pull down the foam into shape, taking tension off the cover itself. This also enables you to concentrate on neatness, pattern symmetry and so on when covering. The calico may either be a continuous piece stretched over a whole seat or back, or in strips, glued to the foam round the edges. The latter is particularly useful if the piece is to be deep buttoned, when lining it all over is not practicable unless lining and cover are put on at the same time.

Another, completely different use for calico is the simulation of hide upholstery. The calico is stretched tightly over a firm foam base and primed with flexible PVA glue or acrylic medium mixed with a dark base colour. Further layers

147

of lighter colours, also rich with PVA or acrylic, are worked in locally to mimic wear, fading and the grain of the leather, and the whole thing is given a clear top coat. Fire-retardant calico is obtainable from upholstery suppliers and from theatre suppliers.

COVERING

With most upholstery the aim is to be neat and tidy, if only so the work will not draw attention to itself. This translates in practical terms into achieving consistent tension when pulling down foam or buttoning, making even and symmetrical pleats around curves, finishing corners neatly and so on. The golden rule in all these is to make temporary – or at least easily reversible – fastenings until you know that something is working. Use skewers or temporary tacks to hold fabric down or pleats in place until you are ready to go round with the staple gun; draw buttons in with slip knots until you are happy that they are even, before tying off with a half hitch.

DROP-IN SEATS

These provide some of the most straightforward work because the edge of the cover fabric is pulled under the seat and the fixings are out of sight.

1. Glue foam to the ply base according to the desired shape and fix polyester wadding to it with a light spray of glue if it is to be used. Ensure that no foam or polyester will be pulled round the edge on to the underside of the base.
2. Cut a piece of fabric – either the top cover, or calico if it is being used – big enough to cover the seat with at least 5 or 6cm (enough to grasp hold of) going round onto the base. Check the alignment of the pile or pattern if there is one.

3. Spread the fabric out face down and position the seat, foam-side down, on top of it. Pull the fabric over the middle of one edge and fix with two or three staples. Move to the opposite side and repeat, putting enough tension into the fabric to stretch it tight and to pull the foam into shape if necessary. Then fix the middle of one of the remaining sides, followed by the middle of the last side, each with moderate tension.
4. Now you will have a cross shape of stretched fabric and four loose corner areas, which can be dealt with separately. Work your way out to each corner, putting a few staples in each side alternately. How close you place the staples will depend on the fabric and on whether you are relying on it to pull the foam into shape; in the latter case aim for one every 2cm or less, and be careful to maintain even tension.
5. At the corners, form pleats to take up the excess fabric. These may be a single pleat on one side of each corner, or 'box pleats' whose two sides meet on the corners. If the pleats are obtrusive, slipstitch them to the adjacent fabric.
6. Another way to pull fabric down over straight edges with even tension is to use a piece of timber or plywood to push the whole edge down at once. A row of close staples is put in without applying extra tension to the fabric. This requires two pairs of hands.

STUFFED-OVER WORK

The term 'stuffed-over' is applied to seats that are built on the chair frame itself, with all or part of the rails being covered, rather than on a separate frame that drops in. It is also used more loosely to describe any piece where nearly all the frame is covered, like a modern sofa.

Stuffed-over seats differ from drop-ins because the fixings of the cover fabric are usually on an exposed surface of the frame, and in that (apart

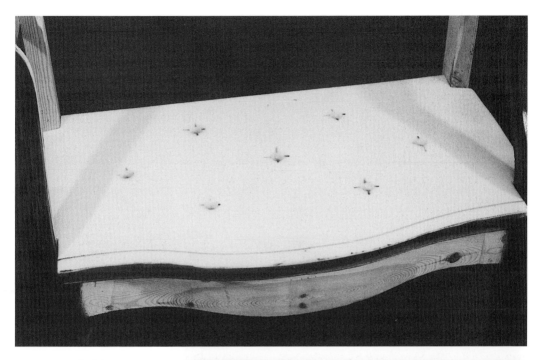

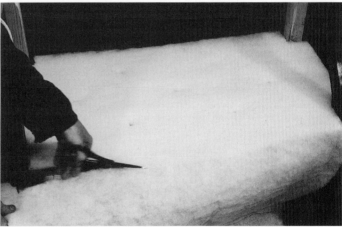

ABOVE: Bevelled foam lightly glued in place on a 4mm ply seat. Buttoning positions already marked and cut.

Trimming polyester wadding in position on the seat.

from on stools) it will be necessary to cut the cover round the uprights of the back (and arms if there are any).

Where the cover fabric finishes on a visible surface, the fixings are placed carefully along a chosen line, the surplus cover is trimmed back just shy of them, and a trimming is used to hide the fixings. Flat braids and gimps, which have enough width, are most easily glued on, either with a hot glue gun, 'Copydex' or a product such as 'Bostik' or 'UHU'. You can also buy 'gimp pins', small tacks with heads in a range of colours

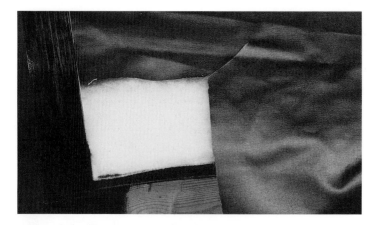

Cover fabric being prepared, showing Y-shaped cut to go round bottom of arm.

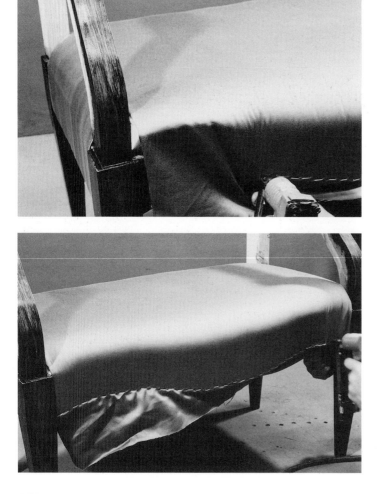

Pulling down the front of the cover fabric.

Finishing pulling down the cover fabric.

that blend into the trim. Thinner trims such as chair cord are more difficult to glue on without mess and are better stitched; others, such as beading or decorative nails, are designed to be hammered on. Nails, of course, can be used to fix the cover, but, if you are using them as a decorative trim over staples, it is more convenient to buy 'nail head trim' – strips of conjoined false nail heads, every fourth one with a hole in it for a real nail.

COVERING CURVED EDGES

Unless your fabric is very stretchy, covering a shape like a scroll or round stool with a single piece of fabric will involve gathering in the fullness of the fabric in a series of pleats or tucks.

Place fixings (skewers, staples or temporary tacks) at wide spacings first, always pulling the fabric at a right angle to the edge you are fixing it to. If you are pulling down foam at the same time, judge the tension by eye and by the feel of the cover fabric. Pull down again in the middle of each gap and place another fixing. Go on placing fixings in the middles of the gaps until you have a row of closely-spaced fixings separating a series of equal-sized gathers. Then fold each of these into a pleat and fasten it down.

Even-pleating depends on the placing of the first set of fixings. On a simple, unchanging curve, they should be equally spaced, but on a curve that gets progressively tighter, the pleats may need to get correspondingly closer together. The spacing of the first fixings must allow

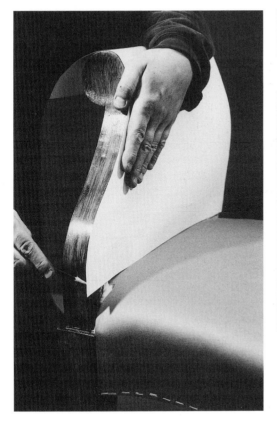

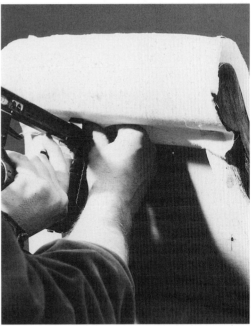

*ABOVE: **Pulling foam round the scroll with a calico strip glued to the last few centimetres.***

Making a paper template of the arm.

151

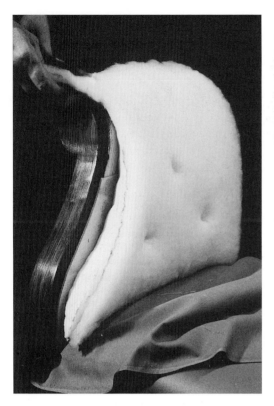

Cutting the wadding for the arms.

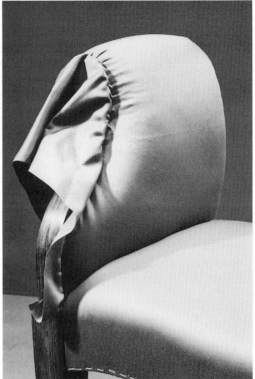

Stapling the arm cover round the scroll – before trimming.

for this, as it will affect the eventual number and placing of the pleats.

BORDERED SEATS

A completely different approach to curved edges, and one that is essential for a feather-edged seat of any shape, is to use a separate border of fabric sewn to a seat piece. For simple seats, it is easiest to make up the cover first on a sewing machine. Carefully make a template of the plan view of the seat, add a small seam allowance and cut it out. Cut a strip of fabric for the border – join two pieces if necessary – allowing a little extra to get hold of when you pull it down and staple it. Pin it to the seat piece and sew together; piping may be inserted at this stage if required. Turn the cover the right way out, pull down over the seat and fix. If the template has been made according to the size of the foam and thin polyester wadding is then wrapped over it, the cover should fit very snugly.

On more complex shapes, it may be easier to join border and seat piece *in situ*. Again, cut a seat piece using a template, adding a couple of centimetres on each edge. Cut a strip of calico 4 or 5cm wide and fix it with a light spray of glue around the top edge of the border area of the seat. Put the wadding in place, lay the fabric for the seat on top and pull it down and pin it to the calico all round. When you are happy

---

Making Piping

---

1. Cut strips of fabric on the bias (at 45 degrees to the weave), wide enough to go round the piping cord plus another 25mm.
2. Join end to end to make a continuous length, and press the joins.
3. Wrap the cord in the strip of fabric, using a zipper foot on a sewing machine to stitch as close as possible to the cord.

---

with the way it is stretched, hand-stitch it to the calico and remove the pins.

Cut a strip for the border as before. Turn over a centimetre or so at the top edge and press it, then pin in place and slipstitch to the seat cover. Pull the border down and fix to the frame. It is possible to incorporate a piping as you sew seat and border together; otherwise a chair cord or some other trim may be stitched on afterwards. Where the top edge of the border is three-dimensional it may not be possible to press in the turned edge before starting to attach it. In this case, cut an oversized piece for the border and pin it in place. Trim it *in situ*, and turn the top edge by hand to fit the seat. If necessary it can be pinned to hold it in shape, removed and pressed.

BUTTONING

Buttoning is a decorative technique derived from old ways for holding covers and fillings in place. It is divided into surface buttoning, which is used to make a more or less two-dimensional pattern, and deep buttoning, which is more three-dimensional. Buttons are usually covered with the same fabric as the upholstery, using two-part 'moulds' or 'cover-buttons'. If you have only a few to do, you can cover them (or any button with a wire loop back) yourself. Cut a disc of fabric about three times the diameter of the

button. Put a running stitch of strong thread around the edge and place the button in the middle; pull the thread ends to gather the fabric tightly round the button and tie the ends. Push on the back of the button if it has one. If you have many to do, it's easier to use the jigs available from haberdashers, or to take your fabric to a commercial button coverer.

Surface Buttoning

It is possible to add surface buttoning after a cover has been fixed down, as long as it is not too tight.

1. Carefully measure and mark out the positions of the buttons with chalk.
2. Using an awl or a thick needle, make a hole in the cover fabric where each button will go.
3. If the support is plywood, drill a 4 or 5mm hole through it for each button; push the drill bit all the way down through the filling and press it against the ply before starting the drill or the bit will tear out a lump of foam.
4. Thread each button on to a length of twine and thread both ends through a large needle. Push the needle down through the filling and through the hole in the ply support.
5. When all the buttons are in place, pull each in turn to the required depth and fix by stapling the twine a few times, or by knotting it round a scrap of wood or fabric.
6. If the support is soft, thread one end of the twine on to the needle, push through the support and filling from the back, and slip a button on. Go back through the same hole in the cover and push through the support just next to the first hole. Fix buttons by knotting round a rolled up 'tuft' of fabric; use slip knots until the button tension is even, then tie off with half-hitches.

Nevertheless, it is easier if the stuffing has been prepared before, as with deep buttoning – there is less pressure on the thread and on the cover fabric.

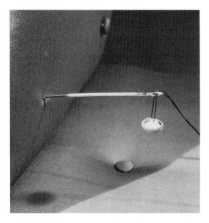

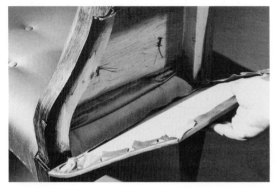

ABOVE LEFT: *Buttoning needle pushed through to pick up an arm button.*

ABOVE: *A small DIY button-covering kit.*

LEFT: *A fabric-wrapped panel covers the outsides of the arms.*

BELOW: *Gluing gimp in place with a hot glue gun.*

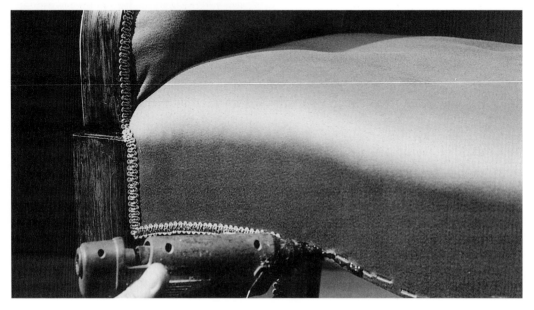

Deep Buttoning

Because it is more three-dimensional, deep buttoning must be planned from the start of the work. Holes must be made in the filling for the buttons to go down into, and the buttons must be put in place before the cover fabric is pulled down. Crucially, the button positions are spaced further apart on the cover than they will appear on the work, giving the fullness needed for the buttons to be pulled down into the filling and for the pleats that are an important part of the visual effect.

First prepare the filling:

1. Cut bevels on back edges of foam and glue to support as normal. The foam thickness should be about half the height of the diamonds in your buttoning pattern. If you want to pull it down with calico at this stage, do it with strips glued along the edges to leave the buttoned area clear.
2. Mark out the button positions on the foam. Carefully measure the distances between buttons and how far they are from the edge, and record on a diagram.
3. Cut a hole about twice the size of your buttons down through the foam to the support. The easiest way to do this is with a length of thin-walled steel tube of the right diameter that has been sharpened on a bench grinder or belt sander. Push the tube hard down into the foam and then twist it back and forth. Make shallow knife cuts in the foam between the buttons where the pleats will go.
4. Drill through plywood supports in the middle of each hole.
5. Lay polyester wadding over the foam and work it into the holes and knife cuts with your fingers.

Then mark up the cover fabric:

1. To each of the measurements between the buttons on the diagram you must add an allowance of around 40 per cent, to allow the buttons to be pulled down into the filling. Whatever this allowance is, add the same to each margin around the buttoning
2. Spread the cover fabric out right side down, and chalk in the centreline. Set out the button positions according to the new measurements and push an awl through each point to make a visible mark on the right side.

Finally, put the whole thing together:

1. Lay the cover in place on the filling. Slip a button on to a generous length of twine, double it and thread both ends through a long needle. Starting on the centreline, pass the needle through a button point, down through the filling and through the hole in the support. Put a rolled-up scrap of fabric between the ends and tie them in a slip knot.
2. Repeat with all the other buttons, working your way out from the middle.
3. Tighten the slip knots to pull all the buttons half way in or a bit more. As the pleats form between the buttons, arrange them to face downwards (on backs) or out towards the edge (on seats); use a wooden mixing stick or a table knife to neaten them.
4. Now fix the cover around the edges. Start by forming the horizontal and the vertical pleats that radiate from the outermost buttons. Pull them down firmly and fix them to the support with skewers or temporary tacks. Then pull down and fix the fabric between them. When you are happy that the tension is even and the pleats are properly placed, go round with the stapler to fix them permanently.
5. Pull the buttons the rest of the way in to their final depth; check that they look even and tie off the slip knots with half hitches. Neaten the pleats again if necessary, cut back surplus cover fabric, and apply a trim to cover the staples if required.

9 PAINTS AND FINISHES

This chapter covers general painting, special finishes such as wood graining and gilding, and the processes by which objects are given the appearance of age. These are areas where a designer may have very specific intentions and ideas. Nearly all props need paint or some other kind of finish applied to them and it will rarely be a single coat of something out of a tin. Most finishes involve a series of layers or processes, as simple as a dirty wash and a little wax polish or as complex as the many layers in wood graining or marbling. A few thin or broken layers work better than a single thick, continuous one; each leaves visi-

A large timber and vac-form picture frame, finished in Dutch metal leaf.

ble something of those which lie beneath. Transparency is achieved by using washes or glazes of thin colour (perhaps partly wiped away) or by spraying or spattering with more opaque paint. Thick paint is reserved for base coats and dry brushing.

A huge variety of materials and technical information is available through the overlapping markets of the decorating business, DIY and the art world. There is also a sizeable market devoted to scenic work. Many books exist on specialist paint techniques, and the Internet offers access to product and health and safety information, technical assistance and much more.

Paints, stains and varnishes are broadly divided into the water-based and the solvent-based. The former means materials which use water as a vehicle, for thinning and for washing brushes, and dry through its evaporation. The latter refers to those where the vehicle or thinner is an organic solvent such as alcohol or acetone, the vapour of which is given off as the finish dries. Water-based materials are therefore safer in this respect (although they may have other more hazardous ingredients) and are used for general work. Solvent-based materials are used when superior performance justifies the extra precautions, or where no water-based option exists.

EQUIPMENT

The most basic equipment necessary, as ever, is a suitable workspace. It will get messy and so should be uncluttered and easy to clean. It needs a large sink and draining board, storage for materials and tools, and enough table and floor space for the work. Mix paints in small plastic buckets and pots from decorators' merchants; for small quantities use paper or polystyrene cups, or a plastic bucket lid as a palette.

Brushes

Basic flat decorators' brushes, either natural or synthetic, are quite adequate for most painting

---

Washing Brushes

The same routine applies to all brushes:

- wipe off any surplus paint with rag or newspaper;
- rinse the brush in the appropriate solvent, ensuring that paint is removed from the tops of the bristles;
- wash the brush in warm, soapy water; rinse thoroughly to remove all the soap;
- shake out what water you can. Shape the damp bristles with your hand and dry the brush by hanging it up or standing it upside down.

Most solvents should not be put down the drain for environmental reasons: bottle the waste and get advice from your local authority on how to dispose of it. If solvents such as methylated spirits are left to stand after use, much of the waste settles as sediment and the solvent may be reused. Hardened brushes can be resurrected with brush restorer or paint stripper, although some of the life will have gone out of them. If you have a strong hand cleaner by the sink, it is worth trying that first.

---

and are available in sizes from 12mm upwards. If you do a lot of figurative work you may want to invest in artists' brushes. Long, fine, flat brushes are better for glazing and varnishing. Small artists' or model-makers' brushes can be used for fine work, while some finishes require specialist tools available from decorators' merchants.

WATER-BASED PAINT

Acrylic Paint

A number of manufacturers offer acrylic polymer paint systems on the scenic art market. Each consists of a range of colours, sold as suspensions

157

Dry pigment supplies.

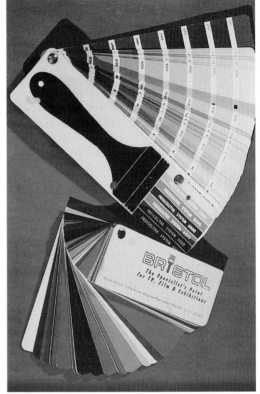

Paint manufacturers' swatch books.

of pigment in a polymer binder and including modern synthetic as well as traditional artists' colours. Densely saturated with pigment, a little goes a long way; they can be thinned simply with water, mixed with polymer media or used to tint emulsion paint or other materials. Prices are high, particularly for strong synthetic colours, and the shelf life of partly-used containers may be short, but these paints are convenient and versatile.

Dry Pigments

These are available from suppliers of scenic materials and (more expensively) art shops. Before use, they need to be mixed with a binder

– some kind of glue to hold the particles of pigment together as a durable paint film. Traditionally, diluted glue size is used to bind pigments for theatrical use, and, although the resulting paint is not completely waterproof, it is certainly economical. Acrylic or PVA media are more permanent and convenient; PVA is the cheaper but it is white when wet and so colours dry differently.

Dry pigments have two advantages over other paints. The first is their much better shelf life: for the pigments this is indefinite, and for dry size or bottled polymer media, very good (although PVA and acrylic emulsions are both susceptible to frost damage). The second is that the pigments

Making Paint from Dry Pigments

The procedure is the same with size and polymer media:

1. Put the required amount of pigment in a suitable container and mix with a small quantity of water to form a thick paste. Some pigments are difficult to mix in – a few drops of methylated spirits or alcohol will solve this.
2. Add the required amount of binder to the paste and mix them together.
3. Gradually add water until the desired consistency is reached.
4. How much binder? Size mixtures for painting should be much weaker than those for gluing or scrimming: 250g of size in 5ltr of water will give a basic binder that can be mixed with pigment/water pastes in equal quantities, before thinning with water. Polymer media vary so much that it is impossible to give figures, but a little goes a long way.

can be used with a wide range of binders, both water- and solvent-based, and for colouring resins, plaster and so on.

Household Emulsion Paint

You can have these mixed in a huge variety of colours, and if you need a large amount of a particular colour (as a base coat, for instance) they are very economical. Books or cards of sample colours simplify matching and ordering, and different finishes are available. Strong primaries are hard to get and the bases contain a lot of filler, so these paints do not intermix well, although they can be modified with dry pigment or acrylic scenic paint. Black and white emulsion can be bought from theatrical suppliers, and white also from DIY or trade outlets, but beware of cheaper paints with poor covering power.

Glazes

The wide choice of water-based polymer emulsion products on the market means that you need rarely resort to traditional, solvent-based versions. Glazes are used to treat paint surfaces to make them uniformly matt or glossy and as a pigment binder, particularly in layers of transparent colour. They also isolate layers of paint in processes where the next one will be partly wiped away, such as wood graining. Harder glazes can be used as protective varnishes when much wear and tear is foreseen. Products vary in price, from simple PVA emulsions (which dry very soft) to hardwearing two-part acrylic systems. The former may need thinning with water to ensure perfect clarity. All can be spoilt by storage at low temperatures, so avoid cheap offers from market stalls.

SOLVENT-BASED MATERIALS

In spite of the widespread availability of water-based materials, there are a few solvent-based products that continue to be used in props work because of their particular properties.

Shellac

This is secreted by insects that have fed on the sap of several Indian trees. It is dissolved in alcohol or methylated spirits to produce a quick-drying varnish widely used for wood finishing, pigment binding, sealing porous surfaces and so on. Large quantities should not be used without ventilation to remove the evaporating solvent. Brushes may be washed in methylated spirits or in a solution of borax in warm water.

French Enamel Varnish

This is a shellac/alcohol mixture dyed to a range of brilliant transparent colours. These can be thinned for use as quick-drying glazes and stains, or used at full strength to paint on glass, clear plastic or metal. They are also used to break down the colour or pattern of fabrics and are particularly effective when sprayed. Once again, effective ventilation is important, especially when spraying them.

Car Sprays

These are aerosol cans of cellulose paint widely used as a convenient, quick-drying spray paint. However, the hazards of the propellant, the paint solvent vapour and the minute droplets of paint generated mean that suitable ventilation and/or protective equipment (respirator and goggles) is needed for these products to be used indoors. As with FEV, their use has declined with increasing safety awareness.

Wood Stains

Sold commercially, these are usually solutions of dye in a petroleum distillate such as white spirit. They exploit the solvent's ability to carry the dye deep into the wood without raising the grain – a problem with water-based stains. Good ventilation hastens drying as well as preventing a build-up of vapour.

Gold Size and Bronze Binders

Both are involved in the production of metallic finishes (*see* below). Traditional gold size is a kind of varnish using petroleum distillate as a vehicle, and some of the best binders for bronze powder use alcohol or cellulose thinners. In both cases water-based alternatives exist which are safer but otherwise technically inferior.

Metal Primers

These are usually solvent based, adhering better to the bare metal and forming a barrier to corrosion. Recently, some water-based primers have appeared on the market; to get the best out of these, degrease the work carefully and allow a long drying time.

Solvent-Based Varnishes

These are generally harder-wearing and more waterproof than their water-based equivalents. Most use petroleum distillate as a vehicle and good ventilation is essential when they are used. Two-part polyurethanes that use an iso-cyanate hardener are more dangerous than single-component versions and should never be sprayed without adequate ventilation and protective equipment.

'FAUX' FINISHES

Wood Graining

Wood graining for the stage ranges from simple treatments that help an otherwise glaring prop to 'disappear', to elaborate processes that set out to mimic the fine timbers of period furniture. It differs from traditional, architectural wood graining when it seeks to portray old or damaged wood, and in that it is usually seen from further away. There is also often good reason to use water-based media only, while traditional techniques rely heavily on the solvent-based. Nevertheless, the wide choice of books and materials that exists for the home improvement market is a good source of inspiration and techniques.

Although there are expensive specialist brushes and other graining tools in the shops, much can be done with ordinary brushes and with cheap or home-made tools. If you are new to wood graining, experiment with these before investing further.

Selecting a Graining Technique

How Many Layers?

Most wood-grained finishes use an opaque base coat covered with one or more layers of broken or more transparent paint that mimic the figure and pore structure of the timber. Layers are often sealed with a glaze to enable subsequent layers to be wiped or combed away more effectively. A simple technique, perhaps

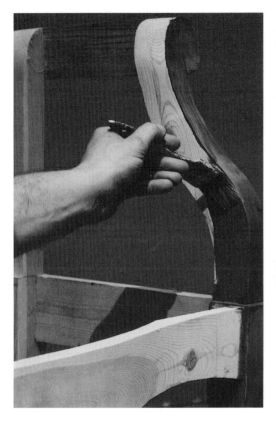

ABOVE: Base coating a furniture carcass.

ABOVE RIGHT: Dragging through the wet top coat with scrumpled greaseproof paper to create a simple wood-grain effect.

Specialist wood-graining tools – two combs, two heart grain rockers and a flogger.

to give anonymity to a piece of background furniture, might involve only a glazed base coat and a top coat wiped or brushed off to give a directional pattern resembling grain. At the other extreme, a finish resembling a specific decorative hardwood might include base coat, separate pore and figure layers, a toning coat to modify colour, several coats of rubbed-down varnish and a polished wax finish – though it is rarely necessary for a finish to be so complex.

Use References

If possible, study real pieces of the wood you want to copy. What is the most prominent pattern or effect? Reproducing this will be the key to your technique. What is the palest colour you can see? This will lead you to your base colour. Build your process by making a series of samples to test colours, techniques and the process as a whole – remember that each layer will be altered by all those that succeed it.

Base Colours

These are usually plain, but experiment with mottling if you can see it in the wood you are copying. Look for the palest colour in the wood and make a base that is slightly paler still (after glazing, if applicable) and slightly brighter in colour. Water-based base colours can be made from white emulsion tinted with acrylic paint or dry pigments, or emulsion mixed in the shop to your requirements, if you have a large area to cover. The consistency should be just thick enough to give opacity without leaving brush marks; often two thin coats are better than one thick one. For fine work, base coats can be rubbed down with wire wool or fine sandpaper to remove any roughness. If you can cope with the fumes and do not mind the longer drying time, eggshell or satin-finish, interior solvent-based paint makes a good, smooth, base coat; you can tint it with dry pigments and it does not need glazing.

Figure

This is the pattern produced in the timber by the way it is been sawn in relation to the annual rings and the ray system, and by the nature of the rings and rays themselves, which are prominent in some species and all but invisible in others. The appearance of both varies according to the way the wood has been cut. On surfaces that radiate from the centre of the tree (quartersawn), rings tend to show as closely-spaced, parallel lines, and rays as intermittent stripes running across the grain. On surfaces at right angles to these (plainsawn) and away from the centre, the rings are broader and more widely spaced, and the rays appear as slashes in line with the grain. Plainsawn surfaces that pass near but not through the centre produce the classic 'heart grain' pattern of irregular interlocking vee shapes.

The bolder ring patterns of plainsawn timber can be painted on with a small brush and broken up by flogging or by dragging through with a stiff dry brush. They can also be made by brushing on paint, wiping with a cloth and pulling a suitable tool such as a rubber comb or a piece of bubblewrap through the thin layer that remains, to leave a suitable striped pattern. For heart grain, a tool known as a 'heel' or 'rocker' can be bought or made. This is a curved surface of rubber or dense foam covered with concentric, semi-circular ribs and is pulled through wet paint to leave a pattern resembling heart grain: this method is faster, though less controlled, than painting it on.

Pore and Fibre Effects

These are the (usually) small-scale patterns of dark and light created by the wood fibres and the pores that enable moisture and nutrients to move around the living tree. In timbers without strong annual rings they may be all that characterizes a timber besides its colour. They may be reproduced in a number of ways. That offering the greatest scope for variation involves painting on a layer of quite thin, transparent colour, wiping it down in the direction of the grain with a rag or dry brush, and then pulling through it with a tool chosen to make the desired pattern. Materials such as scrumpled paper, plastic or fabric, steel wool, pot scourers, fine rubber combs and bubblewrap all leave distinctive patterns. A single pull will leave a different pattern to many, especially if the angle of each pull is slightly varied; pulling

Dragged effects – scrumpled paper.

Pot scourer.

Rubber comb.

Heart grain rocker.

The need to drag through at the end of each stroke requires planning and careful use of masking tape if more than one grain direction is involved.

Three-dimensional graining, using thick, coloured Idenden and a large homemade rocker.

smoothly gives a different effect to a hesitant or shaky action. A minority of timbers show a pore pattern both with and at right angles to the grain, which may be mimicked by wiping the paint at right angles before pulling something coarse through in the direction of the grain, or by pulling through with the grain while the paint is fresh, and then again at right angles when it is nearly dry.

Other techniques include: streaking the wet paint layer with a dry brush before flogging it (this gives a subtle pore pattern without remov-

ing much of the paint), or finely splattering the paint on and then flogging or dragging it to elongate the droplets in the direction of the grain.

METALLIC FINISHES

The need often arises to give a prop (or part of one) a metallic finish, either to persuade an audience that the object is made of metal, or simply in imitation of a traditional finish, such as the gilding on a period picture frame. A number of metallic finishes are in common use.

Metal Leaf

The brightest of all, effectively a continuous layer of polished metal. Available in only a few colours, although these can be modified in a variety of ways.

Metallic Pigments: 'Bronze Powders'

These are dusted on to a tacky surface and buffed, or mixed with a binder to produce a brilliant but short-lived paint. Their brightness derives from the fact that they are actually tiny, flat wafers of metal.

Ready-Mixed Metallic Paint

Available in many forms, these are the most convenient but the dullest of the metallic finishes,

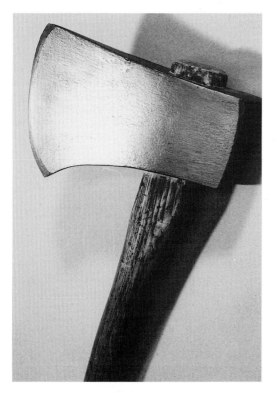

Wooden axe blade treated with graphite powder in PVA.

with an acceptable shelf life at the expense of brilliance. 'Silver' and 'gold' sometimes look more like metallic grey and beige. Useful when that is all that is required, or as a base for another finish.

Powdered Graphite

Mixed with shellac, PVA or wax and rubbed or painted on, this buffs up to a rich lustre resembling old polished iron or steel. The less binder involved, the brighter the effect and the more likely it is to end up on the performers' hands. This is not a very permanent finish, particularly with wax, and may need frequent renewal.

Metal Powders

Not to be confused with metallic pigments, these finely-ground, pure metal powders are mixed with polyester, urethane or epoxy resin and painted into a mould as the first layer of a cast. The dull-coloured cured mixture is brought to a bright metallic finish with wire wool, abrasive paper and metal polish. Not really a surface-coating technique, this is dealt with in Chapter 6.

Background Colour

Broken or partial metallic effects over a selected background colour are far more common than total coverage. The choice of background has a strong effect on the finish, contributing colour, age or style; the same metallic finish will look very different over black than over burnt sienna or pale blue. Traditional base colours for gilding were chosen to bring out the colours of real gold and silver and are important to the feel of period work. Scarlet, red ochres or earthy greens are common under gold in furniture; paler bases such as raw sienna, yellow ochre or chrome yellow are common in architectural work. Silver was and is most often applied over greys and blues.

The use of black or dark brown as a base, particularly when the recesses of a moulding or relief are left dark, emphasizes age. More 'theatrical' effects come from brighter, multi-coloured backgrounds. When choosing base colours bear in mind that layers on top of the metallic finish, such as glazes, will affect the background. Always try to produce samples before deciding on a process.

Working with Metal Leaf

Effectively attaching a very thin sheet of metal to a surface, metal leaf produces the brightest finishes. And, while other finishes become dull and muddy if worked into, leaf will shine up through layers of stain or glaze; it can be wiped or cleaned back to its original brilliance for highlighting (or for starting again). Real gold or silver leaf may occasionally be used, but they are beaten so thin that handling them is slow and skilled work and

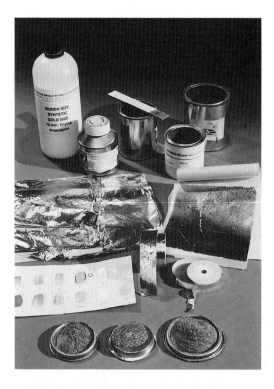

Gilding materials – sizes, powders, loose and transfer leaf, and ribbon leaf.

their use will not be described here. 'Dutch metal' and aluminium, respectively, are usually substituted and are thicker and much easier to apply, to the extent that much of the process can be done with clean fingers. Dutch metal is an alloy of copper and zinc and a small range of colours is available. The most common (No. 2½) is similar to 22 carat gold; on stage, a warmer grade containing more copper is often useful. Aluminium leaf is invariable in colour and a poor imitation of real silver; it is generally true that bright silver finishes are more difficult to achieve than golds. Pure copper leaf is also available.

Metal leaf comes either 'loose', which is best for intricate, three-dimensional surfaces, or 'transfer' – backed with tissue paper for quick and easy application to relatively plain ones. It is usually supplied in 140mm squares, in quantities ranging from 25-leaf 'books' to packs of thousands. Transfer leaf is also available as 'ribbon gold', rolls of continuous leaf in a variety of widths.

Applying Metal Leaf

Techniques for applying metal leaf fall into two groups: water gilding and oil gilding. The former is a slow and skilled process usually used with precious metals on luxury items and has little application in theatre work. Oil gilding is much faster, and uses a coat of a 'gold size' – a varnish-like coating, drying to a tacky surface to which the metal adheres. Traditional gold sizes are based on linseed oil (hence the term 'oil' gilding) and are rated from '1 hour' up to '24 hour' – the nominal time before they are ready to gild on to. 'Japan size' is a solvent/varnish mixture that dries even faster than 1-hour oil size. The slower the size, the finer the metal surface produced and the longer the 'open time' – the window of tackiness during which the leaf can be applied. These all wash up in white spirit.

There are also water-based acrylic sizes that dry in minutes and have an almost indefinite open time. They are economical and easy to use but they do not self-level and are prone to frothing if too vigorously applied. Since they never completely harden, they are unsuitable for objects that will be handled, whereas oil sizes become quite tough after a suitable drying period. For the ultimate resistance to wear use epoxy resin: experiment to find the right moment to start applying the leaf.

The basic process for applying Dutch metal, copper or aluminium leaf is as follows:

1. *Prepare the surface and apply background colour.* Metal leaf faithfully reproduces every detail of the surface to which it is applied, and careful preparation is needed to achieve the smooth, polished surface of traditional gilding. Wooden surfaces can be painted with several coats of coloured gesso or a shellac/pigment mixture; both can be rubbed down with fine steel wool to a silky finish and conveniently combine surface preparation with background colour. Wood that has been already painted or primed can be rubbed down or flow-coated with a self-levelling resin or varnish. There is no call to go to this trouble if the surface already has a texture that suits your purpose. The only absolute requirements are that the surface should be dry and neither absorbent nor greasy, so bare wood will need some kind of priming, and metal or plastic surfaces may need to be washed to degrease them for the gold size to stick.

2. *Apply the gold size.* Paint on a thin, even layer with a soft brush. Be careful not to leave puddles, which will take longer to dry. The leaf will stick only where you put the size. Wait for it to reach the right state of tackiness: faintly sticky when touched with a fingertip or knuckle but leaving no residue on the skin. How long the size takes to reach this state will depend on what you have chosen, from a few minutes for acrylic-based products to 24hr for a slow oil size – it is important not to start applying the leaf too soon. Some water-based sizes have a bluish tint when wet that disappears when the size is ready to receive the leaf.

3. *Apply the leaf.* If working with loose leaf, lay pieces on to the tacky size and settle each one down gently with your fingertips. A clean, dry brush may help on intricate surfaces. Try not to touch the size with either fingers or brush. Do not press hard at this stage; do not worry about the overlaps (these are removed later); and do not worry about small gaps, even if you are aiming for a total coverage.

Laying in Dutch metal leaf.

Settling the leaf gently with an old duster.

Polishing in the leaf, and skewing away overlaps, with the duster rolled into a tight nib.

The aim is to get the whole surface covered rather than to concentrate on one small area. If you are after a particularly broken effect, try tearing the leaf into small, random pieces and distributing them to your liking. If working with transfer leaf, press each piece into the size and rub the back of the tissue paper with your finger or a burnishing tool before peeling away the paper.

4. *Fill in the gaps.* Inspect the surface for gaps and fill them with small pieces of leaf. If blanket coverage is your aim, this will be the slowest part of the process; one way to speed it up is to dust the work with a powder of the same colour as your leaf, if one is available (*see* the section on metallic pigments below). With broken effects, half close your eyes or view the work from a distance so that over-large gaps stand out.

5. *'Polish in' the leaf.* Use a piece of soft, dry cloth to press the leaf firmly into the size. Fold it into a small, tight 'nib' to get into tight corners.

168

The finished frame.

BELOW: *Modifying the appearance of leaf: with dark, dyed shellac...*

...and with pale matt emulsion worked into the corners.

Progress from an up and down dabbing action that sticks the leaf down to vigorous side-to-side rubbing that polishes the leaf and breaks off the overlaps. If you try to fill gaps at this stage, you may find that the polishing has robbed the size of its tack; you will need to apply more where necessary and wait for it to dry. Dutch metal and copper leaf both tarnish with age and aluminium becomes duller. Subsequent processes such as tinting or ageing also serve to protect the leaf; but, if it is to be left bright, a thin layer of shellac or animal glue will to prevent tarnishing at the expense of a slight loss of brilliance. However, the timescale of much theatre work is such that the problem does not arise.

169

Using Metallic Pigments

Metallic pigments, or 'bronze powders', may be used in two ways: dusted dry over one of the many types of gold size (*see* above) or mixed with a binder to make a paint. A wide choice of colours is available, and they can be inter-mixed. Small amounts of dry colour pigment may also be added; for example, bright aluminium powder makes a more convincing 'steel' if modified with a little black.

Dry dusting is a traditional method for filling in small gaps in gold-leafed work, and it is usually

LEFT: *Dusting dry bronze powder into tacky goldsize.*

BELOW: *Stippling black emulsion into the bright gold surface...*

...and rubbing away again with a cloth.

possible to obtain a powder the same colour as the leaf you are working with. It is also a finish in its own right, producing an even, all-over coverage quickly on intricate surfaces. The effect is more satin than the high lustre of leaf, although it can be polished up a bit with a soft cloth. Broken effects are hard to obtain on flat surfaces, but mouldings or carving can be highlighted by loading up a piece of upholstery foam with powder and printing it on. Surface preparation and gold-size application are the same as for leaf, and the powder is applied with a soft brush or felt or foam pad. Whichever is used, there is a tendency for the powder to become airborne; a mask and goggles should always be worn and the work done where the 'fallout' can easily be cleaned up.

The use of bronze powders 'wet' involves mixing them with a binder that will hold them together when the work is dry. Thick, viscous binders produce the brightest effects as a layer of metal floats on the surface, the tiny flakes aligned by surface tension. Applying the mixture quite sparingly, with almost a dry-brushing technique, works best. There are many proprietary binders. Those based on cellulose lacquer are bright and quick-drying (if you have only a tiny area to do, clear nail varnish works as well as anything); the solvent is acetone (or nail-varnish remover). Japan goldsize and purpose-made acrylic or shellac products also work well, washing up with white spirit, water and methylated spirits, respectively. 'Gold' pigments are mostly bronze or brass and many will react with ad hoc binders such as PVA glue or button polish: you may return from lunch to find your gold has gone green or blue. These mixtures are acceptable if you can get them on to the work and dry before the reaction takes place. 'Silver' pigments are aluminium, and a reaction called 'gassing' occurs if they are mixed with water, with potentially explosive results if the mix is stored. They should therefore be used with one of the solvent-based media.

For small-scale work, mix as you go: use something like a discarded plastic lid as a palette, pour a little puddle of binder on to it and deposit some pigment next to it. Dip the brush in the binder, then in the pigment and apply it to the work. For detail or line work keep alternating binder and pigment; if dry-brushing, visit the binder often.

Mix up a pot-load only if you have a large area to do quickly. Premixed metallic pigments always seem to look muddier – the object is to get a layer of metal to sit on top of the binder, and the more thoroughly they are mixed, the less likely this is to happen.

Metallic pigments can be very effective in combination. A deep gold, or one with some dark pigment added to it, is laid in first and a medium gold dry-brushed into it; finally the highlights are picked out with bright, pale gold.

Lastly, pigments can be applied with wax polish and buffed lightly. Subtle blends and ageing are possible because the wax remains workable and can be polished away; for the same reason this is not a very permanent finish.

THE AGEING PROCESS

Some kind of treatment to give the appearance of age is essential to many prop makes. A long list of expressions is used to refer to such treatment, such as 'breaking down', 'distressing' and 'antiquing'. For some people they are interchangeable, while for others each has a specific meaning. The important point is to make sure that you understand a designer's requests: discuss the progress of the work in concrete terms, if possible with samples or references.

Sometimes the purpose of this work may be to enrich by giving a sense of history, to draw attention to age. More often, these processes are used to make something 'disappear' – a freshly painted object stands out, while an old one recedes into the background, its significance (if any) absorbed subliminally. Both demand a

Techniques

Dirt washes and glazes: a simple way to take the edge off the newness of something is to give it a wash over with a dirty or contrasting colour. If applied to an absorbent surface such as bare wood or over fresh, matt, emulsion paint, the mixture can be kept very thin; over glazed or non-absorbent surfaces it will need more binder to help it to stick. Brushing on a layer of weakly-pigmented 'glaze' and then immediately and selectively wiping it away again leaves the dirt colour in those hard-to-clean corners but removes it from more exposed parts. A little of this technique goes a long way – it is easier to add more than to take it off after your chair has dried looking as if it has been dipped in farmyard slurry.

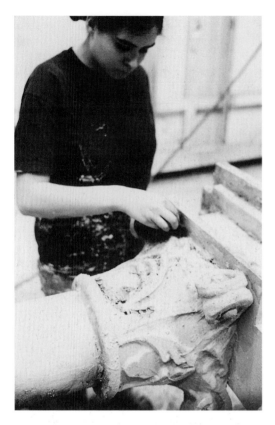

Working a dirty wash into the corners of a carving.

familiarity with the ways in which materials age and a sense of what is appropriate in a given situation in order to work well.

Age shows in many ways and the passage of time affects materials differently. Colours fade; dust and grime accumulate in corners. Objects in frequent use become polished or worn. Silver tarnishes black, iron and steel rust, and copper, brass and bronze corrode to greens and blues. Indoors, wood tends to darken; exposed to wind and sun it is bleached to silver-grey, and the soft grain deteriorates faster to leave the hard grain in high relief. Paint and varnish crack, peel, flake or blister.

Rust is iron oxide that forms on iron and steel on exposure to water or atmospheric moisture. The red and yellow earth pigments are themselves produced by iron oxide and accurately represent the range of colours shown by rust. When new, it is the colour of yellow ochre or an ochre/raw sienna mix; as it ages it passes through burnt sienna or red ochre (classic rust) to colours as dark as burnt umber or Indian red. It is best to use more than one, a lighter one on top of a darker colour, lightly stippling on a thick mixture with an old brush or a scrap of foam. The trick is to avoid leaving repetitive patterns – stand back to check and modify anything that catches the eye. If you want the encrusted effect of severe rusting for an audience at close quarters, build up a texture with sawdust and glue before painting.

Patination of copper or bronze can be produced by an adaptation of the rust and glazing techniques described. The colours produced by natural corrosion range from pale blue to mid-green, while the chemical patination applied to bronze sculpture and fittings is usually a deep translucent brown. The former can be applied as a base coat and highlights or worn areas picked out with bronze powder; the latter are best done as glazes over leaf or another metallic finish.

Corrosion on these metals is generally less 'crusty' than on iron and steel.

Cracking and peeling effects can be achieved in a number of ways. Smearing a little Vaseline into corners before painting enables the dried paint to be rubbed away easily. Painting on a layer of thin latex, allowing it to dry and painting emulsion on top produces a finish easily worked with a wire brush to a broken, textured surface.

Proprietary crackle glazes cause emulsion paint films laid on top of them to break up into bold crack patterns, while crackle varnishes produce subtler effects reminiscent of ageing ceramics.

Last but not least, plain 80-grit sandpaper, either manually or under power of some kind, can be used to erode paint, wood, fabrics and many other materials to great effect.

ABOVE: **Crackle glaze on a wooden moulding.**

ABOVE RIGHT: **Crackle varnish on a chaise leg – altogether more subtle than the preceding figure.**

Using a palm sander to physically distress a piece of 'leather' luggage.

GLOSSARY

Absorption casting
A way of making thin-walled casts, in which a porous mould (usually plaster) absorbs liquid from a suspension of the casting material causing a deposit of it to build up against the face of the mould. Used with natural and synthetic latex, other polymers and clay.

Acrylic
A polymer used to make clear plastic sheet (perspex, for instance). A water-based emulsion is used as glaze and as a paint binder.

Alginate
A very fast-setting, non-toxic, flexible mould-making material used in life casting and for making quick, single-use moulds.

Alpha gypsum
Type of plaster calcined (roasted) under pressure; it requires less water for mixing than beta gypsum or alpha/beta mixtures, and is also stronger and more expensive.

Anti-rake
To build or adjust a piece of furniture or scenery so that, when placed on a rake (q.v.), it still has true verticals.

Arc
(i) Part of a circle or (ii) electric arc produced when a current is made to jump a gap between two solid conductors; used as the heat source in many welding processes.

Architrave
Architectural element spanning the tops of columns. Any timber moulding used around a door opening.

Armature
Framework or other internal supporting structure for clay modelling.

Astragal
Small timber moulding much used in panel mouldings.

Bead
Small convex shape running along a moulding or round a turned object.

Beadfoam
American name for expanded polystyrene.

Beta gypsum
Type of plaster calcined at normal atmospheric pressure. Weaker and less expensive than alpha plasters and requires more water to set properly.

Billet
An uncut block of polystyrene from the manufacturer's mould; usually 8ft × 4ft × 2ft (2,440mm × 1,220mm × 610mm); sometimes bigger.

Binder
Anything used to hold pigment together in a paint film after the water or solvent has evaporated.

Blank
Block of material from which an object is to be turned, carved or machined.

Brazing
'Gluing' metal parts together with molten filler alloy, without melting the parts themselves; similar to soldering but carried out at higher temperatures.

Break down
To modify a new-looking surface with dirt or damage to give an appearance of age.

Breakaway
Intended to be broken as part of the action.

Bricklaid
Built up from small blocks of a material glued together like bricks.

Bronze powder
Metallic pigments made of microscopic wafers of metal, usually a type of bronze or brass; used for gilding and making metallic paint. A wide range of colours is produced by heat or chemical treatment.

Brown foam
Rigid polyurethane foam made by mixing two components; used, for example, for light-weight castings and backfilling vacuum-formed mouldings.

BS 476
British Standard relating to the flammability of building materials.

BS 5852
British Standard relating to the flammability of upholstery and furnishing fabrics.

Butt joint
Joint in which the parts are simply brought together to be screwed, glued or welded, rather than overlapping or interlocking in some way.

Button polish
Heavy, deeply-coloured shellac varnish.

Calico
Cheap cotton fabric like light, finely-woven canvas; mostly used in upholstery and softs (q.v.); flame retardant grades are available.

Cast
Object made in a mould; to make an object in this way.

Catalyst
Substance added to a resin to start the reaction that cures it.

'Celastic'
Material resembling stiffened felt that can be softened by dipping in acetone; used for masks and puppets, for instance.

Centre punch
Tool used to indent steel before drilling – marks the centre indelibly and prevents the drill bit from slipping.

Chipfoam
Reconstituted foam used where a very dense foam padding or filling is required. Also called recon.

Chopped strand mat
Form of glass-fibre reinforcement made of short bundles of fibres lying in all directions, held together with a binder.

Class 0
A Class 1 material that also passes certain tests in BS476 Part 6.

Class 1
Applied to materials that pass tests defined in BS476 Part 7 Class 1, relating to the surface spread of flame.

Clear
Of timber: without knots. Of resins and glazes, for example: transparent when set.

Colloidal silica
Amorphous silicon dioxide, also known as fumed silica. Very lightweight powder used to thicken resins, plaster and paint.

Composite
A structural material that combines two or more different materials, usually including a fibrous reinforcement and a material gluing it together. Paper and GRP are synthetic composites; wood is a natural one.

Contact adhesive
Adhesive which is spread thinly on both surfaces to be joined and left to dry; when they are brought together a strong bond is formed on contact.

Core
Rough carving or construction covered with another material for detail, texture or strength.

COSHH
Control of Substances Hazardous to Health.

Costing
Process of calculating or estimating the cost of work; document resulting from this process.

Costume prop
Item attached to or worn as part of a performer's costume.

CSM
Chopped strand mat.

Cutting fluid
Liquid flooded over work as a coolant and lubricant when cutting or machining metal.

Cutting speed
In machining, the relative movement of a tool in relation to the work that works best for a given material.

Cyanoacrylate glue
Commonly called Superglue.

Degrease
Wash with a detergent or solvent to remove grease, before painting or gluing.

Demould
To remove a cast from a mould. 'Demould time' is the length of time between casting and demoulding.

Dextrin
Modified starch used, for example, to make paste, improve surface hardness in plaster.

DFR
Durably flame retardant; flame-retardant treatment that will survive the wetting or washing of the fabric.

Die
Tool used to cut a thread on a metal tube or round bar.

Distress
To give an impression of wear and tear by physically damaging or eroding something.

Dressing
Stuff spread around a setting to add detail once it has been fitted up.

Dutch metal
Gold-coloured alloy of copper and zinc.

Earth clay
Natural, water-borne clay.

Emulsion paint
In Britain, a water-based, polymer-bound paint for interior decorating. Used for priming and for large areas of flat colour. Called latex paint in the USA.

Epoxy resin
Thermosetting resin used as an adhesive, for making GRP and as a hard-wearing glaze.

EPS
Expanded Polystyrene.

ERW
Electrical Resistance Welded; lightweight steel tubing made by folding sheet steel and welding it along its length.

Exotherm
The heat generated by the reactions involved in the setting of plaster, the curing of resin, and so on.

Face veneer
Surface layer of plywood or blockboard, sometimes decorative.

Fence
On woodworking machinery, a guide which stock is held against or slid along.

FEV
French enamel varnish (q.v.).

Filler
A product for filling holes or textures in wood or metal; a powder mixed with resin to thicken, colour or add bulk to it.

'Fimo'
Polymer clay brand.

Fixture
A simple jig for speeding up a particular operation on a woodworking machine.

Former
Part of a construction cut to a particular profile, usually used in multiples to hold other parts in that shape; for example, the discs at the top and the bottom of a cylinder, a shape used to bend something round, or to hold it in shape while it is glued.

FRA
Fire Retardant Additive.

French enamel varnish
Shellac varnish coloured with dye; a range of strong colours is available and can be intermixed.

Gas welding
Oxyacetylene welding (q.v.).

Gauge
A device for marking or measuring a set distance; the thickness of wire or metal.

Gilding
The process of covering something with metal leaf or metallic paint.

Gimp
Type of braid often used to trim the edges of upholstery and mask the cover fixings.

Gluegun
Electric tool to melt sticks of thermoplastic glue, allowing it to be squeezed out by thumb or trigger action.

Gold size
A water or solvent-based product painted on to an object to be gilded, producing a tacky surface to which the leaf or powder will adhere.

Graphite
Powdered grey crystalline form of carbon used to create 'metallic' effects and as a releasing agent in white metal casting.

GRP
Glass-reinforced plastic: a composite made of glass fibre embedded in (usually) polyester or epoxy resin.

GSMA
Gas-Shielded Metal Arc; MIG or MAG welding (q.q.v.).

Hand prop
A small prop carried on by a character; usually retained by the performer during a show.

Hardwood
Timber from broadleaved trees (for example oak, ash or mahogany).

Hessian
Sackcloth – strong, open-weave jute fabric.

Hog ring
A metal band closed with a special tool, used for joining expanded metal sheet.

Hot wire
A tool for cutting polystyrene which uses a resistance wire heated by a suitable low-voltage current.

HSS
High Speed Steel; used to make drill bits and tools that can be run at higher speeds than standard carbon steels.

'Idenden'
Proprietary brush-on insulation material widely used in the theatre for producing textures and for covering polystyrene; hard-wearing and fire retardant.

IFR
Inherently Flame Retardant; implies something made of a non-flammable material.

Jig
A device made to hold or move material in a controlled way to perform a specific operation on a woodworking machine; a former used to bend a particular shape in metal, for instance.

Jute scrim
Loose, open-weave jute fabric used for reinforcing plaster; also called plasterer's scrim.

Kerf
The width of the cut made by a saw; to bend wood by making a series of closely-spaced saw cuts in it.

Laminating
Sticking layers together; combining glass and resin to make GRP; forming curves in timber by gluing together several thin, flexible layers.

Latex
Natural rubber; and the white milky liquid that dries to form it.

Latex paint
In the USA a water-based, polymer emulsion decorating paint.

Lathe
Machine that rotates stock while a tool is applied to it, making shapes with circular cross-section.

LEV
Local Exhaust Ventilation. General term for fume or dust extraction. Hazardous airborne substances are sucked away and filtered or released elsewhere; there may also be a supply of clean air.

Life casting
The process of taking moulds from parts of the body and casting from them.

MAG
Metal Active Gas; welding process similar to MIG (q.v.) but in which the shielding gas reacts with the weld pool.

MEKP
Methyl Ethyl Ketone Peroxide; the most common catalyst for polyester resin.

Metal powder
Finely-powdered metals, mixed with resin and polished after curing to resemble the metal.

MIG
Metal Inert Gas; welding process in which a metal wire provides both the arc and the filler metal and the weld pool is shielded by inert gas; see also MAG.

'Milliput'
Modelling compound based on heavily-filled epoxy resin.

MMA
Manual Metal Arc; welding process in which a flux-coated metal rod provides both the arc and the filler metal and the weld pool is shielded by gases emitted by the flux as the tip of the rod melts; also called arc welding.

Model
The designer's scale model of a set or part of it; someone from whom life-cast moulds are taken; to make something in clay or similar plastic material.

Modelling wax
Modelling medium based on wax. Becomes completely liquid when heated; can be painted on to work or melted out of moulds.

Mould
A three-dimensional 'negative' of a shape in which a cast is made.

Moulding
The process of making a mould; a strip of timber with a decorative or non-rectangular profile; a decorative profile in architecture.

MSDS
Material Safety Data Sheet; gives technical information about the composition of a product, hazards, control measures and dealing with spillage. Should be available for any product, but you may have to contact the manufacturer for a copy.

NDFR
Non-durably flame retardant; flame-retardant treatment that will not survive the wetting or washing of the fabric.

Ni-chrome
Nickel Chrome. Most common alloy for making resistance wire; used in hot wire cutters.

Nominal
Of measurements, those conventionally used to describe an object but which are not technically accurate. For example, sawn timber described as 1in by 3in, or 25mm × 75mm may vary in actual size and, when planed down to a particular size (say 20mm × 70mm) is still described by the original nominal measurements.

Oil clay
Dried earth clay mixed with oil and grease to make a modelling medium that will not dry out or shrink; becomes very soft when heated.

Oil-based
See Solvent-based.

Open time
After applying glue to something, the length of time available in which to bring the parts together.

Original
An object from which a mould is made.

Oxyacetylene welding
Welding process in which the heat comes from burning a mixture of oxygen and acetylene, the filler from a metal rod and the weld pool is shielded by controlling the oxygen content of the flame.

PAR
Planed all round; all four surfaces of a length of timber have been planed.

Parting agent
Release agent.

PAT testing
Portable Appliance Testing; regular electrical safety testing for tools and anything else that can be plugged into the mains.

Pattern
Object used to make a series of moulds or to check the shape or measurements of others.

Pearl glue
Animal glue supplied in small pellets, traditionally used as a wood glue; now used more for scrimming, paint binding and retarding plaster.

Piece mould
Mould made in a number of sections to avoid undercuts (q.v.).

Pilot hole
A small hole drilled before using a screw, tap or larger drill.

Plastazote
Strong, flexible, closed-cell foam in various colours and thicknesses, used, for instance, for puppet making, structural costumes and padding.

Plaster
In prop making, usually means fast-setting products based on plaster of Paris.

Plaster bandage
Open-weave cotton fabric coated with fast-setting plaster; used for life casting, covering polystyrene and sealing plaster moulds.

Polycaprolactone
Low-temperature thermoplastic which can be modelled with bare hands.

Polyester resin
Thermosetting resin used for making GRP and for small, solid casts.

Polymer clays
Modelling products based on synthetic polymer compounds and plasticizers, usually hardened irreversibly by baking.

Polymer plaster
Plaster mixed with a cross-linking polymer emulsion instead of water.

Pouring gate
Channel provided in a mould through which to pour in a liquid casting material.

PPE
Personal Protective Equipment (goggles, gloves, for instance).

Practical
Functioning: a practical gun must go 'bang', and a practical tap provide water; non-practical ones are not required to.

Press-mould
Simple mould made by making an impression of an object in a slab of clay.

Process
One or more of the steps involved in making an object.

Props list
Any list of the props required for a show. Some scripts contain a list and stage managers may extract it before rehearsals begin. The designer often compiles one that refers to the particular production and during rehearsals stage management will use detailed lists to track acquisitions. A maker's list is usually of the specific items they are responsible for.

Pulling down
Stretching and fixing an upholstery cover over a filling.

PVA
Polyvinyl Acetate. Most often found as a white, water-based emulsion, used, for example, as wood glue, glaze and paint binder; also used in solvent as a release agent.

Rabbitskin glue
Expensive form of animal glue used in traditional gilding processes and for painting on cloths that must retain their flexibility.

Rake
A sloping area of floor, either part of a set or a whole stage.

Recon
Reconstituted foam used where a very dense foam padding or filling is required; also called chipfoam.

Rehearsal prop
A stand-in or dummy prop used in rehearsals; in the case of furniture, it may itself be a make, so the dimensions are consistent with those of the actual item.

Release agent
Substance used to coat an original or a mould to prevent a mould or a cast from adhering.

Resincloth
Old generic term for 'Celastic' or 'Samco'.

Ripping
Sawing along the length of a piece of wood, in the direction of the grain.

Risk assessment
An examination of the hazards and likelihood of exposure to them in a particular process, in order to ensure that it is acceptably safe to perform. Any routine process involving potentially hazardous materials or equipment should be the subject of a formally recorded and regularly reviewed assessment; all new or unusual processes should also be assessed.

Roughing
In turning, the process of reducing square stock to a cylinder; in carving or modelling, initial work producing basic forms.

RTV
Room Temperature Vulcanizing.

Runner
Channel connecting the pouring gate of a mould to the mould cavity itself.

Running prop
Prop consumed in the action, such as a cigar or a breakaway item, or that is perishable and needs to be replaced.

'Samco'
See 'Celastic'.

Sample
Trial piece of work done to test a process or for a designer to approve or select from.

Sawn
Of timber, unplaned, straight from the saw.

Schlag
Imitation gold leaf.

Scrim
Any thin, open-weave fabric, but usually muslin or cheesecloth for covering polystyrene, for example, or jute scrim for reinforcing plaster.

'Sculpey'
Polymer clay brand.

Sheet materials
Any timber-based material in sheet form, such as plywood or MDF.

Shellac
Substance exuded by insects, dissolved (usually in alcohol) to make a fast-drying varnish.

Sightline
Line defining the limits of the audience's view.

Silicone rubber
Synthetic 'rubber' mould-making material for making flexible moulds.

Size
Animal glue, basically low-grade gelatin. Used for priming, scrimming, retarding plaster and as a paint binder.

Skin mould
Mould made using a thin layer of a flexible mould material (usually silicone or urethane rubber) supported by a rigid outer layer (usually plaster or GRP). Essential for large work; done for reasons of economy with smaller moulds.

Skin ply
Thin plywood that can be bent to form curved surfaces, once used for aircraft skins. In Britain usually refers to 1.5mm birch ply.

Slip casting
See Absorption casting.

Slush casting
Way of casting in which a small quantity of casting material is placed in the mould, which is then rotated to cover the inside surface evenly. Rotation continues until the material starts to set. Several layers may be needed to get the desired wall thickness.

Softs
Textile-based props: cushions, banners, for example.

Softs room
Clean area equipped for making softs.

Softwood
Timber from coniferous trees.

Soldering
Joining metal parts together with molten filler alloy, without melting the parts themselves; similar to brazing but performed at lower temperatures.

Solvent-based
Dissolved or suspended in a solvent other than water, or requiring one for cleaning up. Also described as 'oil-based'.

Spigot
Cylindrical form on the end of (for example) a turned item, fitting into a socket on another piece.

Spile
An object that is run around something to keep a pencil a particular distance away from it, to draw an offset line.

Spindle
A thin, turned part in a chair back.

Splayed
Angled cut or construction in wood, as opposed to square.

Spline
A springy, flexible ruler that can be bent through several points to draw a curve through them.

Spring-back
The tendency of a piece of steel to bounce back after being bent around a former; hence the need to make formers slightly tighter than the desired curve.

Starch paste
Wallpaper paste, flour and water paste; used for binding paper pulp or sticking paper together.

Stock
The raw material from which something is being made.

Stop
Object fixed or clamped to a machine to slide stock up to, to enable multiples of the same length to be cut.

'Styrofoam'
A brand of extruded polystyrene; also used in the USA to mean expanded polystyrene.

Sugarglass
Implies a breakaway 'glass' object such as a bottle or windowpane. Once actually made of sugar, now synthetic.

Superglue
Cyanoacrylate glue.

SWG
Standard Wire Gauge: a measure of the thickness of wire, also used for metal sheet.

Table
Flat supporting surface on a woodworking machine.

Tack weld
Small, preliminary weld made to align parts or control distortion.

Tap
Tool for cutting an internal thread.

Thermoplastic
Used to describe a material that becomes soft when heated and hardens again as it cools.

Thermosetting
Used to describe polymers that harden (usually irreversibly) when heated.

Thixotropic
Flowing only when pushed, like margarine.

TIG
Tungsten Inert Gas: welding process in which the arc comes from a tungsten electrode, a separate rod supplies the filler and the weld pool is shielded by inert gas.

Transparent polish
Light-coloured shellac varnish.

Turning
Process of shaping an object on a lathe; an object shaped this way.

Two-part foam
Rigid or flexible polyurethane foam made by mixing two components.

Undercut
Feature of the shape or texture of an object that would prevent it from being easily drawn out of a rigid mould.

Urethane resin
Thermosetting resin used mostly for small, solid casts.

Urethane rubber
Synthetic mould-making 'rubber' closely related to urethane resin.

Vacuum forming
Way of forming objects from thermoplastic sheet by heating it, stretching it over a mould or former and evacuating the air between them.

Vent
Small channel in a mould to allow air to escape as the mould is filled.

Waste mould
A mould that is broken away to remove the cast; usually plaster, but might also be alginate, gelatine or a clay press-mould.

Water-based
Dissolved or suspended in water, or requiring water for cleaning up; containing no other solvents.

White glue
Once meant library paste or dextrin paste, now nearly always means PVA glue.

XPS
Extruded Polystyrene.

FURTHER READING

There are relatively few books about prop making. The three listed below are the most useful. The Motley book, although out of print, is well worth tracking down (through your library or second-hand on the internet); it contains many insights into the essence of the job, as well as practical information.

James, T., *The Prop Builder's Molding and Casting Handbook* (F&W Publications, 1989)

James, T., *The Theater Props Handbook* (F&W Publications, 1987)

Motley, *Theatre Props* (Studio Vista, 1975)

As for books about specific crafts, materials and techniques, there are plenty. I list here only a tiny selection that are particularly useful. The trick when researching a material or technique is to work out who uses it: thus detailed information about epoxy resin can be found in books about boat-building, or white metal casting in those about making model figures.

Baygan, L., *Techniques of Three Dimensional Makeup* (Watson-Guptill, 1982)

Blaikie, T., and Troubridge, E., *Scenic Art and Construction* (The Crowood Press, 2001)

Carter, P., *The Backstage Handbook* (Broadway Press, 1994)

Duginske, M., *Band Saw Handbook*, (Sterling, 1989)

Gordon, J. E., *Structures* (Penguin, 1991)

Holcombe, C., *An Introduction to Woodwork* (The Crowood Press, 2000)

James, D., *Upholstery: A Complete Course* (Guild of Master Craftsman Publications, 1999)

Mills, J. W., *The Technique of Casting for Sculpture* (Batsford, 1990)

Noakes, K., *The Fibreglass Manual* (The Crowood Press, 2003)

Pain, F., *Practical Woodturner* (Unwin, revised edition 1990)

Pritchard, D., *Soldering, Brazing, and Welding* (The Crowood Press, 1997)

Rossol, M., *The Artist's Complete Health and Safety Guide* (Allworth Press, 1990)

Sharpe, M., *Plaster Waste Moulding and Life Casting* (Alec Tiranti, 1990)

The internet, of course, is an enormous and expanding resource for all kinds of information. Manufacturers' sites provide technical information, safety data sheets and practical advice about their products; public bodies and trade institutes post guidelines on safety and best practice. Suppliers can be found and orders placed. Innumerable hobby and craft sites offer information about different techniques, and pictorial references have never been easier to find. Here is just a sample of useful sites:

www.twi.co.uk 'The world's most extensive online source of information and advice on welding and joining of engineering materials'.

www.sculpt.com The Compleat Sculptor, New York sculptor's supplier: online catalogue, technical support, conversion tables and more.

members.aol.com/jrogersgrp/mask.htm
James Rogers' very detailed and well-illustrated account of modelling an oil-clay mask, making a plaster mould and casting with latex.

www.matweb.com Huge database of engineering materials and their properties, searchable by type, trade name, manufacturer, and so on.

www.netic.com.ar/sculp/schaz.htm Useful article on the hazards of common sculpture materials and processes.

www.rosco.com Product information, extensive technical notes, and data sheets for their scenic paints and other products.

www.resin-supplies.co.uk Site of ABL (Stevens) Resin and Glass, UK-based GRP materials supplier: product information, technical tutorials, and so on.

www.smooth-on.com Extensive site of resin and rubber manufacturer: masses of technical and safety information, details of distributors and excellent mould-making tutorials.

www.hse.gov.uk Health and Safety Executive site: UK safety information.

www.polymerclaycentral.com Large hobby site: all you need to know about polymer clay materials and techniques.

List of Suppliers

Theatrical Hardware and Supplies, Prop Making and Painting Materials

Flint Hire and Supply
Queens Row
London
SE17 2PX
Tel: 020 7703 9786
www.flints.co.uk
sales@flints.co.uk

Brian Joseph Hardware Co
Scenery House
2 Hereward Road
Tooting
London
SW17 7EY
Tel: 020 8767 2887

Brodie and Middleton
68 Drury Lane
London
WC2B 5SP
Tel: 020 7836 3289
www.brodies.net
info@brodies.net

Timber and Plywood

Jewson
Arthurs Bridge Wharf
Horsell Moor
Woking
Surrey
GU21 4NP
Tel: 01483 715371
www.jewson.co.uk

S. Silverman & Son (Importers) Ltd
Stirling Way
Borehamwood
Herts
WD6 2BP
United Kingdom
020 8327 4000
www.silverman.co.uk

Timbmet Oxford
PO Box 39
Chawley Works
Cumnor Hill
Oxford
OX2 9PP
Tel: 01865 862223
www.timbmet.com

Moss and Co (Hammersmith) Ltd
104 King Street
London
W6 0WQ
Tel: 020 8748 8251

Steel

Hub Le Bas
Rose Street
Bradley
Bilston
West Midlands
WV13 8TT
Tel: 01902 493506

B&S Steel Supply Ltd
Unit 1
Field End
Ruislip
Middlessex
HA4 6UW
Tel: 020 8842 4855
Fax: 020 8842 4832

Parkside Steel
Units 7–8
Mowlem Trading Estate
Leeside Road
London
N17 0QJ
Tel: 020 8808 1484
www.parksidesteel.com

MODELLING, MOULD-MAKING AND CASTING SUPPLIES

Alec Tiranti
70 High Street
Theale
Reading
Berkshire
RG7 5AR
Tel: 0118 930 2775

Alec Tiranti
27 Warren Street
London
W1T 5NB
Tel: 020 7636 8565

Pottercrafts Ltd
Campbell Road
Stoke on Trent
ST4 4ET
Tel 01782 745000
www.potterycrafts.co.uk

Canonbury Art Shop
266 Upper Street
Islington
London
N1 2UQ
Freephone: 0800 975 5964
Tel: 020 7226 4652
Fax: 020 7704 1781
(Jesmonite, urethanes, painting materials)

4D modelshop
151 City Road
London
EC1V 1JH
Tel: 020 7253 1996
www.modelshop.co.uk
(Huge range of materials for small-scale model-making)

Bentley Chemicals
Rowland Way
Hoo Farm Industrial Estate
Kidderminster
Worcestershire
DY11 7RA
England
Tel: 01562 515121
www.bentleychemicals.co.uk
info@bentleychemicals.co.uk
(High-performance casting and mould-making materials)

Atkins
Atlas Wharf
Berkshire Road
London
E9 5NB
Tel: 020 8533 3499
www.atkinsinsulation.co.uk
(Plasters, silicone and urethane rubbers)

Techsil Ltd
30 Bidavon Industrial Estate
Waterloo Road
Bidford on Avon
Warwickshire
B50 4JN
Tel: 01789 773232
www.techsil.co.uk
(High-performance casting and mould-making materials)

Paper Clay Products
Unit E
The Blacksmiths Shop
Pontrilas
Herefordshire
HR2 0BB
01981 240427
www.paperclay.co.uk
(Dry paper pulp)

Brian Jones and Associates
Fluorocarbon Building
Caxton Hill
Hertford
SG13 7NH
01992 553 065
www.brian-jones.co.uk
(Polycaprolactone)

GRP MATERIALS

ABL (STEVENS) Resin & Glass
8 Zan Industrial Park
Crewe Road
Wheelock
Sandbach
Cheshire
CW11 0PR
Tel/Fax: 01270 766685
www.resin-supplies.co.uk

GRP Material Supplies Ltd
Alchorne Place
Burrfields
Portsmouth
Hants.
PO3 5QU
Tel: 01705 677940
www.grpms.co.uk

POLYSTYRENE

Excel Packaging and Insulation Ltd
Unit 9
Harefield Road Industrial
Estate
Rickmansworth
Herts
WD3 1PQ
Tel: 01923 770247

Service Trading Co
57 Bridgman Road
Chiswick
London
W4 5BB
Tel: 020 8995 1560
(Hot wire equipment)

UPHOLSTERY SUPPLIES

Pentonville Rubber
104/106 Pentonville Road
London
N1 9JB
Tel: 0207 837 7553/4582
www.pentonvillerubber.co.uk
(Foams)

Brimlake Ltd
Unit J5
38–40 Upper Clapton Road
London
E5 8BQ
Tel: 020 8806 4599
www.alltextiles.co.uk
(Fur fabrics)

Creative Beadcraft Ltd
20 Beak Street
London
W1R 3HA
Tel: 0171 629 9964
www.creativebeadcraft.co.uk

Whaleys (Bradford) Ltd
Harris Court
Great Horton
Bradford
West Yorkshire
BD7 4EQ
Tel 01274 576718
www.whaleys.co.uk
(Fabrics)

MacCulloch & Wallis Limited
25–26 Dering Street
London
W1R 0BH
Tel: 020 7 629 0311
www.macculloch-wallis.co.uk
(Haberdashery)

J. D. McDougall Ltd
4 McGrath Road
London
E15 4JP
020 8534 2921
(Fabrics)

SM Upholstery Ltd
212a Whitchurch Road
Cardiff
CF14 3NB
Tel: 029 2061 9813
www.smupholstery.fsnet.co.uk
(Foams and supplies)

Porter Forster
3 Imprimo Park
Lenthall Road
Loughton
Essex
IG10 3UF
Tel: 020 8418 1100
www.porterforster.co.uk
(Large trade supplier of foams, fabrics, sundries and tools)

PAINTING AND FINISHING MATERIALS

The Gilders Warehouse Ltd
Units 5 & 4D
Woodside Commercial Estate
Thornwood
Epping
Essex
CM16 6LJ
Tel: 01992 570453
www.gilders-warehouse

Foxell & James Ltd
57 Farringdon Road
London
EC1M 3JB
Tel: 020 7405 0152
Fax: 020 7405 3631

Atlantis Art Materials
7–9 Plumber's Row
London
E1 1EQ
Tel: 020 7377 8855

Leyland SDM
43/45 Farringdon Road
London
EC1M 3JB
Tel: 020 7405 8985
www.leylandsdm.co.uk

INDEX

190